Quiet Your Mind

A MEN'S GUIDE

Quiet Your Mind

A MEN'S GUIDE

Practical Techniques
to Stop Overthinking and
Take Charge of Your Life

JETT STONE, PHD

ZEITGEIST · NEW YORK

Published in the United States by Zeitgeist™, an imprint and division of Penguin Random House LLC, New York.
zeitgeistpublishing.com

Zeitgeist™ is a trademark of Penguin Random House LLC.
ISBN: 9780593886410
Ebook ISBN: 9780593886212

Cover design by John Calmeyer
Cover art © by Shutterstock/Trutta
Interior design by Katy Brown
Author photograph © by Cara Paiuk
Edited by Sarah Curley

Printed in the United States of America
1st Printing

To my dad.

Your kind heart, steady hands,

and remarkable focus

transformed countless lives.

You inspire me to help others.

Contents

Introduction

When I mentioned writing this book to my close friend, his response said it all: "You're helping men get over sh*t?"

Yes. Pretty much. In these pages, you'll find science-backed and field-tested practical methods to "get over" endless thought loops and ease anxiety, regain confidence, and recover lost time.

My path to this book began many years ago, at my enormous public high school, inside cramped ice hockey locker rooms. These competitive environments revved the engines of my motormouth mind. Back then, when my thought patterns would swerve me into ditches of self-doubt, I didn't have the know-how to course correct. I pressed on, keeping my inner struggles concealed.

Fast-forward many years to my training in clinical psychology, and it was clear I wasn't alone. Everyone seemed to succumb to the habit of overthinking, even the most cool-headed among us. But as I worked toward my PhD, I found myself alone in a different way—as one of the only young men in courses, research groups, and clinical training. Social norms often dictate that men "grin and bear" their internal struggles; our line of work and job status seem to matter more than our inner workings. I felt that my field of study (applying psychology to help real people) risked losing step with the men in our rapidly changing world. This is why I formed a psychotherapy practice designed for men who are hesitant about self-exploration—the guarded, competitive guys I once sat shoulder-to-shoulder with as a kid.

Over the last decade, I've worked across hospitals, clinics, and private practice, and I write about men's mental health for *Psychology Today*. My mission is to tailor psychological science to the nitty-gritty of what sons, brothers, husbands, fathers, stepfathers, and grandfathers feel, do, think, underthink, and overthink. This book is an extension of that pursuit—to help make mental wellness apply to your life and resonate with who you are. Packed with practical tools and insights, this book is your guide to quieting your mental noise so you can achieve your full potential.

What Is Overthinking?

Overthinking refers to unwanted, unproductive, repetitive thoughts. According to the pioneering rumination scholar Susan Nolen-Hoeksema, our thoughts can be directed to the uncertain future, leading to worry. Or they can dwell on past events or failures, leading to rumination. Worrying ("What if?") treats events as if they're controllable; it intensifies our anxiety. Rumination ("Why?") treats events as if they're *un*controllable; it can drag us deeper into depression. Worriers prep for threats; ruminators seek insight. Worry and rumination aren't always distinct processes. They tend to interact and can show up across many mental health issues that people face.

Overthinking isn't always a bad thing. For example, maybe you just received a promotion and you're thinking a lot about your new responsibilities. But the impact of overthinking is most evident when it ambushes you. Thoughts of failure, inadequacy, or regret can be unpleasant and difficult to control—for example, if you're fixated on the possibility of fumbling in your new job.

Who Is Affected by Overthinking?

Overthinking is sneaky. Sometimes you're very aware of it; other times, not.

Jon Acuff, author of the book *Soundtracks*, commissioned research that revealed that 9,950 of 10,000 people, 99.5 percent of participants, struggle with overthinking.

The good news is that your rapid-fire mind slows with age. According to Nolen-Hoeksema, the percentage of people who identify as "chronic" overthinkers decreases from 73 percent of 25- to 35-year-olds to just 20 percent of 65- to 75-year-olds.

We know that men's overthinking can have oversized consequences, from irritability, aggression, and impulsivity to risk-taking, drugs, alcohol, excessive video gaming, and addictions to porn. Some men "lead lives of quiet desperation," in the famous words of philosopher Henry David Thoreau. The CDC reports that males comprise 50 percent of the US population but, tragically, account for 80 percent of deaths by suicide.

Men are often more depressed and anxious than they will admit. We're often taught to avoid burdening others. We get gridlocked when attempting to translate our internal feelings into words. While staying "strong and silent" under pressure saves lives under some circumstances, in others, it's hazardous to our own lives.

Common Causes of Overthinking

Overthinking originates from caring deeply. But when you're too focused on finding solutions or beating yourself up about mistakes, it becomes an unhelpful fixation. It may originate in genetics, childhood adversities, temperament, or personality structure, and it may be influenced by cultural expectations and social norms.

Nearly anything can launch you into a dangerous mental loop: unmade decisions, random thoughts, concerns about "fitting in." Email, social media, and news headlines are designed to be addictive: they hijack your dopamine system, keeping you predicting, modeling, and second-guessing. Research suggests that a tendency to draw negative conclusions from ambiguous information ("interpretation bias") heaves you into spin cycles of worry and rumination.

The overthinking process is akin to a "mental habit loop": a compulsion that's difficult to recognize in action. This idea has been highlighted in the research of psychologists Edward Watkins and Susan Nolen-Hoeksema, and psychiatrist Judson Brewer. Humans are unique creatures capable of complex language, a superpower we instinctually use to ward off uncertainty, fill our knowledge gaps, and avoid discomfort. Our word-producing minds crank up worries and cause us to chew on regrets.

Over time, this process becomes deeply grooved. It operates beneath our conscious awareness, becoming a habitual response to certain stimuli, like lying in bed the night before big meetings, comparing prices online, or staring at a blank document and a blinking cursor under a tight deadline.

OVERTHINKING AND THE CYCLE OF STRESS

Stress is a general response to demands that strain your body's natural capacities. It's an alarm system that alerts your brain and primes the rest of your body to deal with challenges and pressures. Most animal species experience stress, and it often motivates action. It can be positive, like when you're exercising and stress increases your heart rate and strategically redirects your blood.

However, stress can be unhelpful when it amplifies overthinking. Stress triggers the sympathetic nervous system, which readies the body for quick action in high-intensity moments, and the adrenal and pituitary glands, which release the hormones that fuel worry and rumination. If you accumulate a lot of stress over time, this "chronic stress" heightens your risk for cardiovascular, digestive, sleep, musculoskeletal, and mental health issues.

Stress and overthinking are connected in a vicious cycle. When you start overthinking, your brain perceives threats and tells your body to react—perhaps by increasing your heart rate or tensing your muscles. This stress response sends signals back to the brain, which interprets these physical changes as further evidence of trouble ahead. This interpretation intensifies your initial overthinking, leading to a more pronounced physical reaction, and so on.

Learning when and how to relax your stress response requires being attuned to the interconnectedness of your mind and body.

The Science of Rewiring the Overthinking Brain

Researchers use different labels to study overthinking, such as "repetitive negative thinking" (RNT), a persistent dwelling on future or past unhelpful thoughts, and "perseverative cognition," a broader term for mental lingering.

Overthinking disrupts how the brain typically processes information. During overthinking episodes, different brain regions and networks are in play. This includes heightened activity in the prefrontal cortex (PFC), often considered the rational-thinking executive of the brain; a lack of "executive control" causes failures to manage or redirect repetitive thoughts. The amygdala is in action, too, and is central to processing sensory information from the environment and body. There's also increased engagement of the default mode network (DMN), a circuit activated when you're lost in thought. When we're managing stress, the brain areas responsible for healthy introspective and reflective activities are less flexible, often causing us to dwell on worst-case scenarios or previous letdowns. Your brain is wired to detect threats and brood. This leads to what psychologists call "negativity bias."

However, neuroscience reminds us that neuronal wiring is plastic—sturdy but bendable with determined effort. That's why your brain's ability to change from experiences is called neuroplasticity. Being aware, open, and willing to

SIGNS OF OVERTHINKING

- Avoiding social interactions
- Ruminating over your place in the world, telling yourself you don't fit in
- Restlessness
- Playing out situations like grades or paydays
- Mental clutter, juggling too many things, the sense you have too many browser tabs open
- Decision paralysis, indecision about looming choices
- Sleep disturbances due to anticipated stress, "Sunday-night scaries"
- Imagining adverse outcomes and worst-case scenarios
- Constantly seeking feedback and reassurance on decisions and communications
- Comparing yourself to others, being overly concerned that you're undervalued
- Romantic insecurities, harboring baseless doubts about a partner's loyalty
- Digital fixation, constantly refreshing emails and social media
- Conversational rumination, replaying past dialogues
- Freezing up in response to texts and emails
- Procrastination, analysis paralysis that leads you to avoid starting tasks
- Imposter syndrome
- FOMO (fear of missing out)
- Anxiety about being included or excluded

embrace the awkward beginner stage of change will inspire your brain's natural ability to adapt and rewire. Practice patience. Be curious. Experiment. This is how you access your brain's natural neuroplasticity and reorganize your neural pathways.

REWIRING TAKES TIME AND PRACTICE

Rewiring your brain requires checking your pride at the door. I'll show you.

Find a pen and paper. Start writing the alphabet as quickly as possible with your nondominant hand—for example, if you're a righty, use your left hand.

Seriously, try it for 30 seconds. Set a timer.

Did that seem like forever?

In the real world, writing with your nondominant hand is a useless skill. But if it were necessary, if you dedicated time to it, letter by letter, day by day, you'd develop muscle memory. In this situation, your brain and body are clumsy dance partners figuring one another out.

The same thing happens when you rewire your brain to rein in overthinking. Compiling the tools that work best for you will take regular practice. Some tools will seem effortless, while others may feel clumsy. But I encourage you to try them all. Soon, you'll assemble a personalized overthinking action plan; eventually, you won't need this book.

How to Use This Book

This book is designed to help you whether you struggle with overthinking occasionally or it bothers you daily.

Your agenda while reading this book matters a lot. If a tool doesn't seem to work for you, don't try to overpower or punish your overthinking mind; that will only set you back. To gain the most from this book, envision yourself as an open-minded explorer. When you stumble upon something new, will you discard it or store it away? Which tools are valuable enough to carry home to your unique life? They don't have to be perfect; they just have to be useful to you. Transforming this tool kit into your *skill set* will take weeks or months, but it'll be worth it.

Chapter one will focus on bringing you into the present moment and responding to thoughts and emotions in healthy ways. Chapter two provides techniques to manage and prepare for stress. Chapter three offers time management strategies, and chapter four focuses on practices to rewire your thought patterns by gaining distance from your restless mind. Finally, chapter five presents common overthinking scenarios from real life and pairs them with the tools you've gained from previous chapters.

Throughout this book, I'll ask you to take notes. You can use an app on your phone, a journal, scrap paper, or whatever you like. To keep it simple, I'll just say "in your notes."

I've tested or applied these methods for managing overthinking in my own life. I also implement them with my psychotherapy patients, who have found them productive. This book is not psychotherapy, but it could be your gateway to that experience.

While you can't escape, overpower, or outthink your overthinking in the long run, in this book you'll see that how you perceive and respond to overthinking can make a world of difference.

Join me in getting to know your closest traveling partner, who's been with you from the start and can't quit you: your inner voice.

CHAPTER ONE

Create Calm

> You cannot solve a problem with
> the same mind that created it.
>
> —*Albert Einstein*

Overthinking can arrive suddenly like a knock on your door at night. Or it can sneak up in a silent fog. Other times, it's a dictator demanding perfection. A 2020 study in *Nature* revealed that adults, on average, have an estimated 6,000 separate thoughts per day. That's infinite fodder for worry and rumination to creep into your mind, whether you're aware of it or not.

The tools in this chapter will help you tame overwhelming emotions and stay in the present moment. With so much behind-the-scenes mental activity, this is no small task.

As you navigate these tools, remember that being swept away by your thoughts, memories, and feelings doesn't mean you're incompetent. Clinical psychologists view overthinking as a form of "experiential avoidance," the habitual attempt to dodge uncomfortable thoughts, memories, or feelings through intense mental analysis. But you don't reach calm with more intense thinking; the first step is balancing your physical state.

CALM DOWN QUICKER WITH THE "CYCLIC SIGH"

TIME: 30 SECONDS–5 MINUTES

Your brain and the rest of your body are constantly communicating through a feedback loop. Consciously regulating your breath enables you to slow down this rapid-fire brain-body interplay.

Neuroscientists in studies published in 2022 and 2023 found that the "cyclic sigh," a.k.a. the "physiological sigh," can be a quick-acting, real-time method of breathing that settles down your internal state. What makes this breathing exercise different from others is the extended exhalation, which slows your heart rate, and the double inhale, which provides more depth to your inhalation and the exchange of CO_2 and oxygen.

NOTES *Perhaps you've tried mindfulness apps or learned exercises such as "box breathing" (inhaling, holding, exhaling, holding, each for four counts). If so, continue to use those. The cyclic sigh works best when you want to calm your internal state rapidly.*

INSTRUCTIONS

1 Sitting down, begin by inhaling through your nose, halfway filling up your lungs. Immediately following this, "top off" this first inhalation with a second inhalation through your nose. As you do this, place your hand on your stomach and feel it expand on your inhale.

2 Next, slowly exhale out of your mouth for about twice as long as your inhale. Feel your stomach deflate with the exhale.

You may feel an effect within moments, but try this for five minutes. Your breathing and heart rate will slow, triggering your parasympathetic nervous system—your body's "rest and digest" mode.

3 As you gradually become more at ease with the cyclic sigh, you can transition this breathing routine into a "body scan," which shifts your focus to body sensations.

As you inhale, imagine sending your breath downward as if traveling from your nostrils and lungs to your feet. Observe any discomfort or tension areas in your body—start with your head and slowly move down to your toes. Just simply notice and allow the sensations to be in the moment as they are. Where do you feel these sensations most acutely?

CATCH YOUR OVERTHINKING AND BREAK THE CYCLE WITH MOVEMENT

TIME: 1–3 MINUTES

When you're overthinking, you aren't always consciously aware of it. It's hard to change what you don't see. So this exercise helps you identify overthinking in action and distinguish it from constructive or helpful repetitive thinking (e.g., reflection, pondering, or problem solving with an outcome).

Once you've determined that your thinking has crossed the blurry borderline into unhelpful territory, physical action or exercise can help restore your body's balance and improve psychological functioning. A 2024 study from Australia and South Africa found evidence that those who are more active and reduce their sitting time tend to dwell on unpleasant thoughts less and manage their emotions better, potentially leading to milder depression. Regular (and even single-session) workouts can help you bounce back from adversity.

NOTES *After you spot your overthinking, it may seem like taking a break and moving your body is "unproductive." The opposite is true. Overthinking is a trap that locks you into a problem with tunnel vision, where you ask "Why?" or "What if?" questions to no end. It may sound too simple, but stepping away to exercise or get fresh air can untangle you from your mind's suffocating grip.*

INSTRUCTIONS

1. MENTAL CHECK-IN

Use these questions to bring overthinking into focus.

Are bothersome thoughts preventing you from focusing or solving problems?

- Yes
- Not sure
- No

Are you struggling to tame your thoughts?

- Yes
- Not sure
- No

Do you notice a spike in bodily activation (e.g., rapid heart rate or breathing, muscle tension, jitteriness, sweating)?

- Yes
- Not sure
- No

2. EVALUATION

If "No" was your answer to two or three questions, you're likely not overthinking. So, no further action is needed; skip to step five. But if your responses to *two* out of three are "Yes" or "Not sure," you might be overthinking.

And that's okay. Move on to step three.

3. NORMALIZATION

Remember, your thoughts are not facts; they're your mind's attempt to manage uncertainty. Your inner voice is not all-knowing.

4. LEVEL OF CONTROL

Are your thoughts related to a situation, event, or outcome you have any ability to change?

A helpful acronym in these situations is IDEAL: **i**dentify the issue, **d**efine the main aspects of the problem, **e**xplore solutions, **a**ct on solutions, **l**ook back and evaluate. Set a timer when you look back and evaluate.

If your answer is *no*, or you're not sure, it's time to get up and move.

Research shows that overthinking makes you more negative and less effective at solving problems. Try getting up and moving and return to solve the problem later.

5. BODY MOVEMENT

Try these ideas or any others that you come up with: go for a walk or run around the block; take the stairs instead of the elevator; stretch; do push-ups, chair squats, or jumping jacks. Consider keeping a set of kettlebells, resistance bands, or a grip strengthener near your work area or wherever you spend a lot of time.

DECODE YOUR EMOTIONS TO FIND THE BEST SOLUTION

TIME: 5 MINUTES

The more specific you are in chronicling your one-of-a-kind emotional life, the more data you possess to help you take decisive action at critical moments. The rich, untapped emotional underworld that operates beneath worry and rumination is full of valuable insights.

In *How Emotions Are Made*, pioneering emotion researcher and neuroscientist Lisa Feldman Barrett writes, "An emotion is your brain's creation of what your bodily sensations mean in relation to what is going on around you in the world." Barrett coined the term "emotion granularity" to refer to the idea of creating a precise vocabulary to differentiate and describe your emotions. This means moving from a vague phrase like "I'm feeling off" to a more specific phrase like "I'm feeling outraged, eager and jumpy, super-nervous about speaking my mind." Getting more nuanced about how you describe your feelings can help you feel less scatterbrained or confused and tee up more tactical solutions for responding. Data has found that under distress, when you tease apart your emotions, you can reduce anxiety and depression; studies have even found that you're less likely to binge drink and aggressively retaliate.

NOTES *Emotions aren't just mental states but built-in barometers for the human experience. Mastering this tool can transform your life and complement the other tools in this book. Take a look at the emotion wheel on page 31 and collect a few labels that fit your overthinking experience.*

INSTRUCTIONS

1. EMOTION TRIGGERS

Identify the specific situations or thoughts that trigger your overthinking. What's the who-what-where-when of your initial physical and emotional response? Jot it down in your notes.

2. GRANULAR EMOTIONS

Use precise language to name multiple feelings, moving beyond general terms like "upset." Combine emotions into "melodies" and notice how loud or soft they are on the intensity dial. You can even combine words like "chill-axed," "rageful at a 10," or "hopeful at a 3."

3. WORD SELECTION

Create a section in your notes for any emotions that resonate with you during your bouts with overthinking. Come back and fill in these notes whenever you practice this tool.

4. ACTION TENDENCIES

Reflect on how each emotion that you selected influences your behavior. For instance, does confusion or numbness prompt you to withdraw or seek reassurance? Does loneliness motivate you to reach out to others or eat unhealthy food?

5. THE FUNCTIONS OF EMOTIONS

Emotions guide your behavior, communicate your needs, motivate your actions, inform your perceptions, and protect your well-being. How are your emotions—including the unpleasant ones, like anxiety and fear—trying to protect you? Zero in on the deeper longings buried beneath these emotions, such as the need to connect, find safety, or seek comfort. This will help you see your emotion's hidden message more clearly. We'll explore this more in Tool 6.

Emotion Wheel

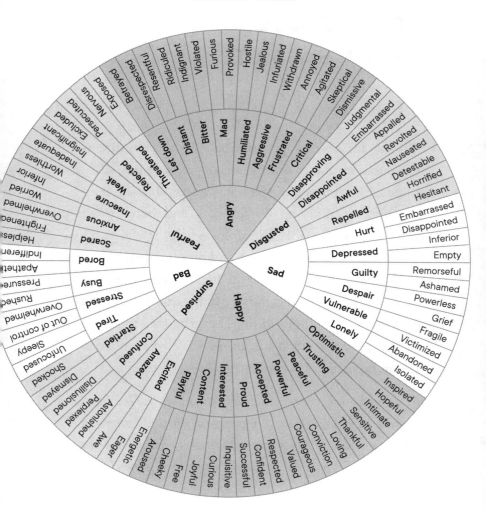

Emotion wheel adapted by Geoffrey Roberts

TOOL ④

LISTEN CLOSELY
TO THE BASSIST

TIME: 2–5 MINUTES

This tool locates the signal through the noise by directing your attention to specific sensory experiences, such as sounds. Research highlights how passive, abstract, repetitive thinking cranks up overthinking, and there's growing empirical evidence that mindfulness helps readjust attention, better manage emotions, and promote psychological well-being. The mindfulness of "focused attention" reduces the wandering of your mind and helps adjust the volume and tempo of emotions during scatterbrained moments. It also lets you slow down and absorb the elements of daily routines or nature that you may take for granted.

NOTES *For this exercise, choose any instrument. One idea is the bass, as you rarely see a bassist positioned at center stage. The idea here is to pay greater attention to the behind-the-scenes elements of life that you might otherwise overlook.*

INSTRUCTIONS

❶ Choose any song you like, but make sure it features multiple instruments.

❷ Select an instrument to focus on. It could be a foreground or background instrument, as long as it blends into the overall sound.

❸ Prepare to listen in a comfortable spot. Close your eyes to minimize distractions if that's helpful. You can practice breathing exercises.

❹ Mindfully listen to the song, concentrating on your chosen instrument. Try to follow it throughout the song and notice when your mind wanders off. That's okay. The whole idea of this exercise is to practice returning your focus to one instrument's sound. You're on the right track if you continuously circle back to your chosen instrument.

❺ Reflect on your listening experience. Was it challenging to keep your focus on just one instrument? Did you notice your attention drifting to more prominent parts of the song?

MAP YOUR ROUTES AND EXITS

TIME: 7 MINUTES

This exercise helps you "map" your frequent overthinking routes. Research has shown that focusing on practical details rather than abstract critical analysis can help reduce the toll of overthinking. You'll be better oriented to problem-solve with a map of the terrain.

Once you've grown comfortable mapping your unhelpful thinking routes, you can take it a step further. Locate an overthinking exit. Gratitude, for example, can reduce the tendency toward worry and rumination. It shifts your focus toward the meaningful aspects of life and enhances your motivating emotions, encouraging a healthier problem-solving attitude.

NOTES *This exercise blends two tools: mapping thoughts and practicing gratitude. They pair well, but you can practice them separately if you'd like.*

INSTRUCTIONS

❶ In the list of common categories and subcategories of overthinking that begins on page 36, circle those that resonate with you.

❷ Are there categories or subcategories not mentioned here? If so, list them in your notes.

❸ Write down your personalized list.

❹ Next time you are in an overthinking episode, practice naming your category. (No judgment. We all have them!) Now, ask yourself: *Is this overthinking route I often take helpful and effective right now?* If it's not helpful, you can follow this up by turning your attention from what you don't know to what you do know: *What are two parts of your life you feel grateful for now? Who has greatly impacted you, and how can you show gratitude to them today?*

Common Categories and Subcategories of Overthinking

PERSONAL PERFORMANCE AND STANDARDS

Perfectionism
Nitpicking imperfections in work or personal life, striving for unattainable standards

Career and Academic Performance
Lack of confidence in performance, academic grades, and future educational paths

Creative Performance
Overanalyzing creative work or artistic value

PRACTICAL AND DAILY LIFE CONCERNS

Health and Fitness
Personal and family health, diet, and exercise routines

Financial Management
Money, expenses, and financial planning

Decision-Making
"Analysis paralysis" in daily decisions; indecision about menu or grocery items or online purchases

Time Management and Productivity
Time use and productivity

SELF-REFLECTION AND IDENTITY

Self-image and Worth
Evaluating personal abilities, appearance, and worth; lack of confidence

Cultural Identity
Fitting or not fitting in to cultural norms

Existential and Philosophical
Contemplating life's purpose and philosophical questions

SOCIAL CONCERNS

Awkward Interactions
Concerns about social judgment or how you're perceived, analyzing social cues, and perception by others, e.g., post-event rumination

Relationship Dynamics
Questioning stability of romantic or other close relationships, including fidelity, or misunderstandings about communication

Parenting
Concerns about your children's safety, health, and parenting decisions

TIME TRAVEL

Past-focused (rumination)
Counterfactual thinking (imagined alternative versions of the past); dwelling on past mistakes, regrets, and "What if?" scenarios. Lamenting or brooding about your failures or your depression.

Future-focused (worry)
Low expectations about the future, rehearsing possible worst-case scenarios about uncertain future outcomes (defensive pessimism), feeling aimless about the future, fears of failure, and over-preparation

VAGUE OVERTHINKING

General Anxiety or Depression
Unfocused worries/ruminations and a general sense of unease that isn't easy to nail down. Loss of control.

WORLDVIEW / EXISTENTIAL

Environmental Issues
Environment and personal impact

Political and Societal Issues
Political situations and injustices

Spiritual or Religious Concerns
Spiritual beliefs and moral dilemmas

Technological
Technology's impact on life and digital security

TOOL ⑥

UNCOVER YOUR DEEPER DRIVES TO FIND CLARITY

TIME: 15 MINUTES

This reflection exercise will connect your overthinking to deeper drives such as belonging, coherence, feeling, orientation, meaning/autonomy, and competence. This activity will help you get out of your head, promote inner calm, and contemplate actions to take. Discovering these deeper drives, or "yearnings," helps organize our mental chaos and translate it into a quest for something more profound.

NOTES *It's easy to forget that overthinking may begin as a constructive endeavor. By endlessly churning your thoughts, you are attempting to protect yourself from pain, and on an even deeper level, you are trying to align your actions with your deeper drives, or yearnings.*

INSTRUCTIONS

Listed on the next two pages are some examples of powerful unmet needs that lurk beneath overthinking.

❶ In your notes, write down each of these drives and give examples of how they may or may not connect to your overthinking pain points.

Belonging: Cooperation is essential to survival. Belonging to a group and knowing that we matter and matter to others is a basic need.

Coherence: We have a fundamental aspiration for aspects of ourselves, others, and the world to experience order, make sense, and be coherent. Yet, sometimes, our lives seem unpredictable or out of order. Our inflexible expectations run up against the reality that life is uncertain or ambiguous and that we don't have a video game joystick to control real life.

Feeling: We spend money on roller coasters for a thrill, watch gruesome true-crime documentaries for horror, and read stories that we know will have tragic, sad endings. Feelings give us vitality. Yet sometimes, we numb or avoid painful internal experiences because we fear they may harm or decrease our ability to function at our best.

Orientation: We are compelled to map out, or at least know, the lay of the land we occupy—a clear sense of where we stand in physical space and time-space. Yet sometimes, we feel lost or disoriented and don't know where we ought to be along our life paths.

Meaning/Autonomy: We want to be the protagonists in our lives and cherish the ability to make our own choices. Sometimes, predefined expectations or other people's beliefs override our autonomy. It's hard to tell what is our dream and what is family's or society's expectation.

Competence: We also yearn to be good at our life's work and excel in meeting expectations and goals. This strong pull to matter and be needed by others for what we know and are capable of can have us striving for impossible standards of perfection.

❷ Reflect on the list of drives you made in step one.

Identify one yearning as your biggest overthinking pain point.

Identify one yearning that you are currently fulfilling.

———————
This exercise is based on Hayes, 2020.

CHAPTER TWO

Minimize Stress

I close my eyes but can't fall asleep, my body
dying for the rest while my mind's wide awake.

—Haruki Murakami, *Kafka on the Shore*

At night, under the cover of darkness, worries and regrets creep in—crawling up, buzzing, tormenting. Next thing you know, you're tossing and turning, your body heat's rising, and even though your body is desperate to rest, your mind's wide awake.

We've all been there.

Overthinking amplifies your sympathetic nervous system, releases cortisol and adrenaline, and keeps you alert—stressed. This chapter's methods are designed to turn short-term stress to your advantage while preventing and managing toxic long-term stress.

While I can offer you tools and techniques in this chapter, I can't personally control your sleep and wake-up times, exercise frequency, social life, or dietary habits— all of which are essential for mitigating harmful long-term stress. A growing body of research reveals how these rising tides are vital to uplifting your cognitive, emotional, and physical health.

CHECK IN WITH YOUR STRESS

TIME: 8 MINUTES

Accumulated over time, stress takes a toll on your body—what scientists call "allostatic load." This tool helps awaken you to your potential long-term stress pain points from carrying this load.

Sometimes, stress operates below the level of awareness until you suddenly fully feel the tension in your clenched jaw from ruminating or drinking alcohol more than you'd like. A 2022 study by researchers in New York and Montreal emphasizes how energy depletion from chronic stress impedes your body's repair and rejuvenation processes. The cumulative effects of stress can raise your disease risk and accelerate aging.

NOTES *Use this simple scale to gauge your current stress levels and consider ways to take preemptive actions. Return to this every few months as a stress check-in.*

INSTRUCTIONS

❶ Reflect on your experiences over the past three months. Using the scale provided as reference, consider each of the following items and write down, in your notes, to what extent you agree or feel they apply to you.

In your notes, track how this sum total changes month to month (and eventually year to year) as you begin to use the tools in this book. Be as honest as you can.

❷ Also, in your notes, jot down potential short-, medium-, and long-term stressors you foresee in the upcoming quarter.

Short-term stressors are temporary physiological and psychological responses to immediate demands, like nervousness before a presentation or navigating city traffic. Remember that these are often helpful for gearing up to answer the bell.

Medium-term stressors are responses lasting days or weeks, often resulting from continuous work deadlines or planning events. This type of healthy stress amps you up to meet *ongoing* challenges.

Long-term (chronic) stressors are prolonged and unhealthy, often due to enduring situations like chronic illness or long-term financial difficulties.

BODY	
MUSCLE TENSION	
0	Relaxed most of the time
1	Occasional tension/discomfort
2	Frequent tightness/discomfort, especially under stress
3	Constant tension, leading to discomfort/pain
GASTROINTESTINAL	
0	Normal function
1	Occasional upset/discomfort under stress
2	Regular digestive issues
3	Severe/frequent problems linked to stress
HEADACHES/DIZZINESS	
0	Rare/never stress-related
1	Occasional in stressful situations
2	Regularly suffer from stress
3	Frequent/intense headaches/dizziness during stress

TOTAL: _____

ENERGY LEVELS AND SLEEP

BEDTIME AND WAKE-UP REGULARITY

0	Consistent bedtime and wake-up
1	Some difficulty with bedtime/wake-up consistency
2	Frequent bedtime/wake-up inconsistency
3	Severe insomnia or sleep issues due to inconsistent bedtime and wake-up (e.g., common in shift work)

FATIGUE

0	Normal energy
1	Some fatigue
2	Regular fatigue
3	Constant exhaustion

TOTAL: _____

COGNITIVE	
CONCENTRATION	
0	Good focus
1	Occasional concentration lapses
2	Frequent difficulty focusing
3	Severe focus issues
THOUGHT PATTERNS	
0	Generally optimistic
1	Some self-critical/unhelpful thoughts
2	Regular self-critical/unhelpful thoughts
3	Persistent negativity

TOTAL: _____

ALCOHOL/DRUGS	
0	No current use of alcohol or other drugs
1	Rare or occasional use of alcohol or other drugs
2	Regular use of alcohol or other drugs but not causing problems in daily life
3	Frequent or problematic use of alcohol or illegal drugs, impacting work, relationships, or health

TOTAL: _____

EMOTIONAL

LONELINESS/ISOLATION

0	Feeling socially connected
1	Some preference for solitude but generally connected
2	Often feeling lonely, less social engagement
3	Strong sense of isolation, numbness, or neglecting relationships

ANXIETY/IRRITABILITY

0	Mostly calm
1	Occasional anxiety or irritability
2	Regularly anxious or irritable
3	Constant anxiety or severe irritability

DEPRESSION/SADNESS

0	Generally upbeat
1	Occasional low moods
2	Frequent sadness, affecting mood
3	Intense depression, impacting daily life

TOTAL: _____

BEHAVIORAL	
IMPATIENCE/AGGRESSION	
0	Typically patient
1	Occasional impatience or agitation
2	Regularly impatient or aggressive, e.g., driving very fast
3	Frequent aggression or severe impatience
ISOLATION/WITHDRAWAL	
0	Regularly social
1	Sometimes preferring solitude
2	Often withdrawing from others
3	Complete social withdrawal

TOTAL: _____

SUM TOTAL: _____

TOOL ②

TRANSFORM PRESSURE INTO BETTER PERFORMANCE

TIME: 30 SECONDS–2 MINUTES

A growing body of research reveals the power of "challenge" mindsets when facing short- and medium-term stressors.

Sweaty palms, racing heart, quickened breath—don't mistake these for weakness or threat; they can be your ally. Practice rethinking nervousness as your fight-or-flight system—cortisol and adrenaline—prepping you for action. By learning to reinterpret your autonomic arousal as your body readying you for a challenge, you can turn these experiences into assets that help you excel under pressure.

This technique is known in psychology as "cognitive reappraisal"; it entails reinterpreting a stressful moment into an empowering opportunity. A recent research review found that positive reappraisal can enhance resilience in stressful situations, and other research has even suggested that adopting a challenge mindset not only changes the perception of stress to be beneficial but also results in healthier cardiovascular responses.

NOTES *This exercise is beneficial when you have spent time preparing for a demanding performance of some kind, but it is less valuable if you procrastinate and don't adequately prepare.*

INSTRUCTIONS

❶ Think of your most recent short-term stressful experience. How did you typically interpret your body's stress signals (increased heartbeat, sweaty palms, muscle tension)?

❷ Identify other upcoming stressors. These include things like crucial meetings, public speaking, and competitive sports events.

❸ As you prepare for your event, and on the day of, coach yourself: "An increased heartbeat, clammy hands, and butterflies in your stomach are signs that your body is gearing up for action and preparing you to be your best." This is an opportunity for growth and to show others what you're capable of. Performance psychologists witness firsthand how mastering this reframe transforms a great athlete into a GOAT.

❹ Choose a phrase, or mantra, that shifts your mindset from threat to confidence. Here are some examples:

- "Pressure is a privilege."
- "This is your time to shine."
- "You are capable and confident."
- "Trust your instincts and let your talent flow."

Who cares if it sounds cheesy at first? Prioritize what works over your ego or feeling silly. You can design your own short, meaningful phrases; practice them in low-stakes situations and then build up to more challenging ones. Paired with paced breathing (slow and controlled breathing), these phrases can help you crush it under pressure.

TOOL ③

PROTECT YOUR WAKE-UP TIME

TIME: 3–5 MINUTES

Reading emails and notifications first thing in the morning triggers your stress response cycle before you're fully awake. By attending to your overstimulating phone first thing in the morning, you squander your brain's wake-up transition (the theta and alpha stages that precede the full beta, wide-awake stage). This daydreamy theta state can be an ideal time to journal or record your nighttime dreams as they are still fresh in your mind.

There's a reason I've asked you to put pen to paper so much in this book! An extensive and growing body of research, pioneered by social psychologist James Pennebaker, has found that expressive writing about stressful or neutral life experiences has broad physical and mental health benefits. For instance, a 2006 experiment out of the University of Texas found that expressive writing prevented depressive rumination among participants who had difficulty expressing themselves.

NOTES *Try this one day per week in the morning, and if it's helpful, begin incorporating it more frequently. Write by* *hand, as it doesn't give you another reason to interact with a phone first thing in the morning.*

INSTRUCTIONS

❶ Tonight, put a notebook and pen near your bed.

❷ When you wake up in the morning, turn off your phone's alarm and immediately put it face down, away from you. Before you enter the online world, grab your notebook. Without judging, without editing, jot down whatever floats from your last dream: blurry images, non-sensical conversations, lingering emotions. Use bullet points, keywords, or messy drawings—it's all good.

You can dream-journal or express anything on the page—the choice is yours. Below are some prompts to get you started.

What's on your mind this morning? Write with honesty. No one will read this but you.

What stresses you out about the upcoming day?

What achievable (real-life) dream do you have, and why is it worth the short or medium stress to get there?

These morning scribbles are a bridge between your sub-conscious and your waking world. Every messy note is a step closer to understanding yourself.

RAISE YOUR STRESS TOLERANCE BY EXPANDING YOUR VISUAL FIELD

TIME: 5–20 MINUTES

When you're stressed, your breath quickens, your heart rate increases, and your pupils dilate. Have you ever noticed how your vision narrows and the world around you blurs in these moments?

Stanford neuroscientist Andrew Huberman describes this as an ancient stress response that locks you into threats to ensure survival. Expanding your visual field can activate your parasympathetic nervous system (rest and digest), reducing stress. If you've ever looked out on the horizon or at a scenic view, you don't need me to tell you that a panoramic view can have a destressing effect.

You can train to raise your stress threshold by consciously putting yourself in uncomfortable situations where you feel stress (exercise or extreme temperatures) and then practicing keeping your mind and body calm under those taxing conditions. Expanding your visual field can work indoors, but it's especially powerful outdoors in nature, whether you're exercising, walking, or just sitting.

NOTES *You may have encountered other methods to build up your capacity for short-term stress, such as cold exposure (ice baths), heat exposure (saunas), or Wim Hof breathing (forced hyperventilation). While effective, these can be costly or carry health risks for some, so it's safest to ask your doctor before trying them. This simpler, free alternative involves using your eyesight.*

INSTRUCTIONS
OPTION 1: DURING EXERCISE

1 Start your workout as usual.

2 As your heart rate goes up, and if it's safe, consciously look around your workout area rather than looking at a focal point straight ahead. The idea here is to train your mind to expand into "landscape" mode and be at ease while your body is under duress.

3 By training yourself to keep a wider view, you can see what's in front of you and what's on your side. Notice how, as your heart beats faster, you can even spot the edges of your own body in your peripheral vision.

4 Maintain this more expansive outlook throughout your exercise. It will associate your body's autonomic arousal with a broader view.

OPTION 2: OUTDOORS

1 If you're indoors, feeling jittery from too much caffeine or exhibiting a short-term stress response, walk outside. Nature is best, but any outdoor space will do.

2 Put away your phone and start walking. You can also play classical music in your earbuds and transform your stroll into a cinematic experience.

3 Begin calming breathing exercises as you walk, focusing on slowing your exhale to reduce your heart rate.

4 Actively change your focus from narrow to wide, trying to observe as much around you as possible. Maintain this panoramic view while walking to help de-stress from overthinking.

TOOL ⑤

HELP SOMEONE ELSE TO DE-STRESS YOURSELF

TIME: 2 MINUTES

Overthinking is a killjoy that pulls you into a narrow visual field of perfectionism, indecision, or overprocessing. But if you can shift your focus from your problems to supporting others in their struggles, you can broaden your perspective and foster deeper connections.

Being kind helps you feel better. A 2016 study in *Clinical Psychological Science* observed how participants' "prosocial behaviors" (helpfulness toward others) reduced their stress levels. More recent research has shown that engaging in prosocial behavior after stress directly lowers blood pressure and pulse, potentially helping mitigate the body's physical stress response.

NOTES *This next activity, a series of questions, is designed to help you decide how you can optimize your helpfulness. Helping someone else de-stress is versatile and can be integrated with other exercises in this book.*

INSTRUCTIONS

1 Assess how you can provide a unique benefit to some-one, such as physical strength, organizing/planning, or cooking? Are you an expert, or do you know a great amount about any area?

2 Look at neighbors, coworkers, kids, parents, or siblings and ask what they're struggling with. Is there someone you know who needs a pick-me-up?

Who is a male friend you haven't spoken to in a while? The unfortunate reality is that men often shed their close friendships over time or store them away until they're abso-lutely necessary.

How much time would it take to text this friend?

3 Brainstorm. Here's an incomplete list of ideas:

Share an uplifting message to a buddy going through a tough time, check in on a guy friend over text, or call someone you feel you are drifting away from. Celebrate someone else's milestone. Give up your bus seat, let some-one go ahead of you in line, thank a service worker, share knowledge about something you learned, leave an encour-aging comment online, leave a generous tip, or pay for someone's coffee. Go out of your way to teach a friend to grill. Lend a genuine ear to a friend's struggles and practice reflecting back what someone's said instead of trying to fix problems.

PREVENT STRESS BY SKILLFULLY ASKING FOR HELP

TIME: 5–20 MINUTES

Humans are wired for cooperation. Quietly and self-reliantly grinding through stress has merit—until you burn out or let others down because you're hauling too much weight. Men are often more likely to choose self-reliance over formal help-seeking, and this is one major contributor to their anxiety. Overdoing self-reliance increases your cognitive load, leading to heightened stress responses or social isolation, which can cue overthinking.

According to 2022 research from Stanford University, others want to offer help more than you realize. Requesting help can even strengthen relationships. People may resist asking for help to avoid inconveniencing others or appearing inferior, needy, or incompetent. Yet this data suggests that seeking advice may increase your reputation of competence.

So, how do you ask for help?

NOTES *According to this same Stanford study, people who can help you are often willing to do so but may be wary of* *invading your privacy or making false assumptions about what you need. Direct requests for help can reduce uncertainty and build closer relationships.*

INSTRUCTIONS

1 Accept that asking for help exposes you to vulnerability. Practice being okay with that. As you learn to adjust your mindset, it's alright sometimes to fake it 'til you make it.

Acknowledge to yourself the potential concerns of appearing weak or burdensome. Like many people, you may worry about being indebted to the helper. Remember: people carry an "over-overestimation bias," which means they magnify the degree to which their requests for support will be rejected.

Reflect on your relationship with help-seeking. Do you typically view seeking help as an admission of inadequacy or a strategic step toward personal growth and development?

2 Be specific and clear about what you need (emotional, informational, or practical support) and why. To tailor your request, consider the potential helper's background, skills, and interests. Is the request reasonable? Use the 10/10/10 Rule: How will you feel about making this request after 10 minutes, 10 months, and 10 years?

❸ Use the opportunity to strengthen your relationship with the helper. Build a rapport through banter. Show appreciation for the help offered. Offer your help in return.

❹ Facilitate the help process by breaking down tasks and providing resources to simplify the helper's effort. Consider the right time, keeping in mind their availability.

❺ Provide feedback on the result, keeping the helper updated on progress.

❻ Reflect. How can getting comfortable putting yourself out there actually reduce overthinking and build a collaborative problem-solving environment? Perhaps you worry you'll be penalized for being "needy" for reaching out at work. What does that signal about your workplace's contagious stress culture? Others probably feel that way, too.

This exercise is inspired by Heidi Grant's Reinforcements, *2018.*

CHAPTER THREE

Manage Your Time

A man who thinks too much about every step he takes will always stay on one leg.

—Chinese proverb

Unstructured time can be liberating, or it can keep you in analysis paralysis, mired in indecision, grasping for your phone, betting on meaningless sports games, sucking you into email-refreshing frenzies, or whisking you down social media rabbit holes. A 2021 study found that the more you engage in repetitive negative thinking, the stronger your feelings of missing out become, which leads you to unhealthy phone behaviors.

This chapter introduces time management exercises to streamline decision-making and avoid procrastination black holes and addictive behaviors. A balanced routine aimed at what truly motivates and matters to you will provide clarity and direction so you don't drain your willpower and motivation.

Experiment with these tools and discover what works best for you.

TOOL ①

ADD UP THE TIME YOU SPEND OVERTHINKING

TIME: DAILY TRACKING
(30 SECONDS PER DAY FOR 1 WEEK)

Let's put a number on how overthinking impacts your time.

This one-time activity is designed to help you bridge the gap between what you're actually doing and what you want to be doing. If you value fitness but frequently avoid exercising, you may experience cognitive dissonance, a mental discomfort caused by the mismatch between your beliefs and actions. Depending on how you deal with it, this discomfort can lead to rationalizations, or it can motivate you.

NOTES *This activity roughly estimates the total time you spend overthinking and engaging in overthinking-related distractions in a week. Your number may be surprising or expected. Either way, use it as motivation to take advantage of your time on Earth.*

INSTRUCTIONS

Track your overthinking episodes and duration in the next week as best you can.

❶ Create a chart like the example on page 68.

❷ For one week, notice each time you catch yourself over-thinking and track it.

❸ Note your distractions: What do you do to distract from the distressing experience of overthinking? (For example, excessive screen time, procrastination with busy work, gambling, or snacking.)

❹ Multiply the sum total by 52 weeks to see a rough esti-mate of what the time you spend overthinking costs you in a typical year.

❺ Write this number down where you can see it, for example, on a Post-it note, and keep it in a place where you will see it every day.

❻ If you could recover this time, how would you utilize it?

Overthinking Time Tracker

Day	Overthinking Instances/ Duration	Overthinking Distractions/ Duration
MON		
TUES		
WED		
THUR		
FRI		
SAT		
SUN		
TOTAL		
SUM TOTAL DURATION		

BLOCK OUT TIME FOR TASKS THAT MATTER TO YOU

TIME: 10 MINUTES

With regular scheduling, you might calendar your appointments or deadlines. With time blocking, you proactively allocate specific blocks of time to the personal and professional—individual work tasks, personal commitments, and even breaks. This allows for more uninterrupted engagement in the tasks you want to prioritize during those time windows.

Time blocking is best when you feel you're juggling responsibilities that make you prone to distractions or seem to follow you throughout your day stressfully. Time blocking allows you to estimate how long a task should take beforehand, makes you more accountable, and allows you to stick to a schedule. It can also ease your work-life balance, ensuring that time is set aside for family matters, financial planning, or passion projects.

Instead of "squeezing in" or sporadically thinking about a meaningful task or project, allocate a specific time, like 8:00 to 8:30 a.m, when your mind is freshest. Once this block is finished, you can smoothly transition to your next task at 8:30 a.m.

NOTES *According to a 2009 University of Minnesota study, switching tasks can lead to "attention residue," where more engaging tasks spill over and disrupt focus on subsequent, less-engaging tasks. To manage this, schedule sufficient time for your most appealing activities after the less-appealing ones to prevent spillover.*

If you're a working dad, especially with young children, or if you have a naturally chaotic, unpredictable schedule, time blocking may not be for you.

INSTRUCTIONS

❶ Identify priorities, beginning by listing all tasks that require your attention. This includes professional responsibilities, personal commitments, and leisure. Categorize these tasks based on their urgency. Label A as most urgent and B as less urgent.

❷ Allocate time blocks for priorities. Start with just one day—tomorrow. Pull up your calendar and assign specific time slots in your day to each task, beginning with the most urgent "A" ones. Depending on your task's complexity, these blocks can range from 15 minutes to several hours.

Reflect on the parts of the day when you typically feel most alert and focused.

Place high-priority tasks during times when you're typically most productive. For many, this might be in the morning, but it could vary.

❸ Implement themed days. Consider dedicating whole days, or smaller blocks of time, like a morning or afternoon, to specific types of work (like admin tasks, home repairs, doctor's appointments for your kids, or creative work). This can help reduce context switching and increase focus.

❹ Incorporate breaks and downtime. Balance is crucial. Schedule short breaks to recharge, including leisure activities like reading, video games, or scrolling.

❺ Set boundaries. For those reserved blocks when you need to get very locked in, inform others to minimize disturbances.

❻ Regularly review and adjust.

SKILL ③

REPLACE BEDTIME OVERTHINKING WITH "CONSTRUCTIVE WORRY"

TIME: 5–15 MINUTES

Sleep efficiency improves next-day cognitive function and energy levels. But daytime stressors can accumulate quickly. Suddenly, the floodgates swing open when you need peace the most—at bedtime. Bedtime is the wrong time to engage in problem solving. This tool offloads concerns and solutions before your mind attempts to do so when your head hits the pillow.

A 2022 meta-analysis in the *Annals of Behavioral Medicine* suggests that overthinking is often a culprit when you have a stressful experience and poor sleep quality. And multiple studies have documented how repetitive thinking impairs sleep quality. Clinical psychologists use cognitive behavioral methods, like "constructive worry," to address prebedtime overthinking. This method involves listing worries and potential solutions well before bedtime, which helps reduce presleep anxiety. This technique can promote quality sleep more effectively than general presleep writing.

NOTES *If your overthinking persists after this constructive worry exercise, read a physical book (with dim light) at bedtime. Don't choose a page-turner or a read that reminds you of your to-do list. Focusing your attention (so your monkey mind doesn't swing from worry to worry) has been shown to help you surrender to sleep.*

INSTRUCTIONS

At least two hours before bed, carve out time to do this exercise. I suggest setting an alarm, as this activity can easily be forgotten.

1 In your notes, create two columns. The column on the left is called "Concerns." The column on the right is called "Solutions." Under the "Concerns" column, write down the specific current problems that have the greatest chance of keeping you awake at bedtime (e.g., *make changes to presentation deck requested by my boss, sign up daughter for summer camp when registration opens at 8 a.m.,* or *was I too harsh to my employee?*).

2 For each concern, decide what next step you can take that may help fix it. Write it in the "Solutions" column. Determine and document whether your solution is a temporary fix, a complete solution, a minor issue to address later, a matter requiring external help, or an unresolved challenge that may have a more apparent resolution in the future (e.g., *time block early afternoon tomorrow to focus on* *the boss's deck, set the alarm 15 minutes earlier to navigate the summer camp registration website,* or *send a text to associate checking in*).

❸ Put this constructive worry sheet somewhere out of eyesight. Simply by doing this exercise, you've managed your problems effectively during productive problem-solving time. Efforts to try again with a foggy, tired mind will be counterproductive.

TOOL ④

STACK YOUR HABITS TO THINK LESS, DO MORE

TIME: 5 MINUTES

Habit stacking is a method for introducing new habits into your daily life. This concept originated with the founder of the Stanford Behavior Design Lab, B. J. Fogg, and it was later popularized in James Clear's *Atomic Habits*. It revolves around pairing new, aspirational habits with an existing, well-established routine.

Fogg's behavior model (FBM) is a widely cited theory that motivation, ability, and prompt must converge for a behavior to occur. When a behavior does not happen, at least one of those three elements is likely missing. Let's assume you are motivated and have the ability but can't find consistency with a new habit. This approach helps you with the "prompt." It simplifies forming new habits by prompting them with routines you already perform.

NOTES *This activity helps you make desirable behaviors more automatic, reduces decision fatigue, and enables you to focus on the tasks that matter to you but are hard to fit into your day, which can lead to nagging guilt and overthinking.*

INSTRUCTIONS

1 Identify a solid, existing habit that you do regularly and that requires little cognitive effort.

2 Next, consider a small but meaningful and manageable habit you want to incorporate—daily to-do lists, physical therapy for chronic back pain, or more gratitude toward people in your life.

3 Combine the two, creating a habit stack. In your notes, write how you will stack your new habit onto the existing one. Link the new habit to the already-in-place routine, creating a sequence. The existing habit acts as a cue for the new one you're attempting to establish. For example, after turning on your computer, spend five minutes writing your to-do list. Or, before getting in the car for work, take two minutes to send a supportive text to someone you care about.

4 For the next week, implement your habit stack. At the end of the week, reflect on the process in your notes. How did it feel to add this to your routine? Was it easier to remember your new habit?

5 If you encounter difficulties, adjust your stack as needed. The goal is to integrate the new habit into your existing routine; with time, it will become seamless.

TOOL ⑤

KNOW WHAT
YOU VALUE

TIME: 10 MINUTES

Overthinking steals your attention in ways that cause you to miss the forest for the trees. When your mind runs amok, getting in touch with what you care deeply about—values—becomes a compass.

Values aren't goals, as they are not achieved. They are closer to directions (like east or west) and are influenced by family, culture, or outside expectations, but only you can choose them. Values are not words from a list; they are a freely chosen way of life. They are also the *quality* of person you hope to show up as in the world.

NOTES *The values domain following comes from the Valued Living Questionnaire, developed by psychologists, which uses an acceptance and commitment therapy (ACT) framework, a psychological approach aimed at helping you accept what you can't change, live in the present, and act according to values.*

INSTRUCTIONS

1 Select a domain that influences your productivity and time management: Relationships, Work & Achievement, Education & Personal Growth, Health & Physical Well-Being, Hobbies & Leisure, Home & Environment, Spirituality/Religion, or Helping Others. Remember, you can revisit this exercise with other domains. Just choose one.

2 Close your eyes and take a deep breath. Reflect on a moment of struggle or failure in this domain area—a tough time when you didn't meet your *own* expectations. Take a minute to reconstruct the scene in your mind's eye: your actions, thoughts, and feelings.

Open your eyes.

What went wrong in that moment? Who was with you?

3 Now, shift to a moment of triumph, empowerment, or deep satisfaction in your chosen domain area. Recall a time when you felt exceptionally competent or fulfilled. Close your eyes and replay this scene.

Open your eyes.

Summarize what was happening in a straightforward phrase, such as "team problem solving," "engaging story-telling," or "connecting with my son."

❹ Mark your qualities. Your greater purpose is often found in triumph and painful moments. Buried beneath the weight of tough times are clues to values.

Using the list on page 80, mark a "P" next to five qualities you lacked during your Pain moment and a "T" next to five you showed in your Triumph moment. Trust your instincts. Overlap of Ps and Ts is okay.

❺ From this list of qualities, pick the top *three* in any category that speak to you the most. Again, go with your gut. You can always revise.

❻ Build your values sentence. In your notes, take time to complete the following sentence using the three qualities you chose. You can create multiple sentences. Keep revising until it feels right.

> "In [*value domain*], I find fulfillment by being [*list 2–3 qualities*] as I [*straightforward phrase of what you were doing during your triumph moment*]."

> EXAMPLE: *"In parenting, I find fulfillment by being attentive, patient, and kind as I teach my son new life skills."*

Once you're satisfied, write it down next to your "overthinking number" from the first exercise.

Personal Qualities

Adaptable	Decisive	Intelligent	Prudent
Ambitious	Dependable	Intuitive	Punctual
Analytical	Determined	Inventive	Reflective
Appreciative	Diplomatic	Kind	Reliable
Approachable	Disciplined	Leader	Resilient
Assertive	Empathetic	Loyal	Resourceful
Attentive	Enthusiastic	Mature	Respectful
Authentic	Fair	Motivated	Responsible
Balanced	Flexible	Objective	Self-aware
Calm	Forgiving	Open-minded	Self-sufficient
Caring	Funny	Optimistic	Skilled
Charismatic	Generous	Patient	Stoic
Collaborative	Genuine	Perceptive	Strategic
Committed	Good-humored	Perseverant	Supportive
Competent	Honest	Persistent	Thorough
Confident	Honorable	Philosophical	Tolerant
Conscientious	Humble	Pragmatic	Trustworthy
Courageous	Independent	Principled	Versatile
Creative	Innovative	Proactive	Witty
Curious	Insightful	Professional	Worldly

SETTLE YOUR MIND WITH MEANINGFUL GOALS

TIME: 5–10 MINUTES

A clear picture of your goals provides purpose and direction and reduces opportunities to ruminate and worry. Now that you've started to articulate your values, you're ready to define your values-driven time management goal.

A 2017 meta-analysis from the United Kingdom explored the impact of goal setting on behavior change, noting the benefits of these factors in enhancing goal-setting outcomes, especially for males: the more challenging goals had a more substantial effect than the easier goals. Goals set publicly were more effective than those set privately. The goals set in face-to-face interactions were most effective.

NOTES *Monitoring goal progress and increasing the frequency of progress monitoring can be crucial in promoting behavior change. Return to this goal-setting activity regularly.*

INSTRUCTIONS

1. DEFINE YOUR TIME MANAGEMENT GOAL

In your notes, write a sentence that begins with, "My goal is to . . ." Then detail a specific and reasonably bold ambition. "Spend more time on tasks that will help me get rich" is vague and not values-oriented, but "beating my record of 50 sales calls this month" is specific and might be oriented to your values.

Ask yourself: *Would my most candid friend agree that this goal is challenging enough and achievable for me?*

2. VALUES ALIGNMENT

In your notes, write down the fundamental values that underpin this goal. Refer to your values statement if necessary.

3. EMBRACE ROADBLOCKS

List any annoying thoughts, beliefs, or past experiences you're prepared to face to achieve this goal. Identify potential unpleasant emotions you are willing to endure. Acknowledge any physical discomforts or sensations you'll likely encounter.

4. THE STARTING POINT

What is the most uncomplicated and feasible first step? Schedule it. Commit to taking this first step on [time, day, date].

5. ACCOUNTABILITY PARTNER

Share and discuss this goal with someone you know
and trust.

6. MILESTONE CHECK

Once a week, rate your progress toward this goal on a scale
from 1 to 5.

- 1 = Not started
- 2 = Just begun
- 3 = Making progress
- 4 = Nearly there
- 5 = Milestone achieved

This activity is inspired by Russ Harris's The Happiness Trap, *2007.*

CHAPTER FOUR

Rewire Your Thought Patterns

I've lived through some terrible things in my life, some of which actually happened.

—Mark Twain

This chapter introduces strategies that elevate you from the front line of your overthinking mind to a quieter, bird's-eye perspective. These new moves will help reshape your thought patterns, offering mental separation that diminishes their intense grip over you.

Psychologists, depending on their area of training, will refer to these methods as "self-distancing" (adopting an outside perspective on oneself), or "cognitive defusion" (targeting your relationship with thoughts). Each makes your thoughts seem less believable and has been shown to decrease activation in brain regions associated with how quickly and intensely emotions get fired up. But learning to de-"fuse" from your inner voice requires some tolerance for frustration and some creativity.

BE YOUR OWN ELITE COACH

TIME: 1–2 MINUTES

Ever notice how you offer kinder, more level-headed support to friends or teammates than yourself? This tool taps into the speech patterns you use when supporting others through challenges.

The next time you're preoccupied with thoughts, try silently addressing yourself in the second person, by name, like a visionary coach. A growing body of research exploring everyday self-talk, led by psychologist Ethan Kross, has found that talking to yourself uniquely alters your perspective, allowing you to interpret adversities as challenging rather than threatening. This shift to "you" (or, in some cases, "we") can also reduce rumination after challenging situations have ended.

NOTES *Begin by practicing this in mildly stressful situations, not overwhelming ones. Build up to more stressful situations. Eventually, this "self-distancing" can help ease your nervousness.*

INSTRUCTIONS

❶ Take a moment to think of a supportive coach, teacher, mentor, someone who's got your back, or even someone you don't know but admire.

❷ Silently coach yourself in the voice of this figure who believes in your ability to rise to the challenge. Extend the support you'd give others to yourself. Speak to yourself as an elite coach would to a promising athlete. What would they tell you?

❸ Label your thoughts as "thoughts." This practice, rooted in the Buddhist tradition, trains you to acknowledge that your thoughts are present without getting caught up in their provocative content. Labeling your thoughts as "just thoughts" can help make them less believable and less powerful.

Here's an example that puts it all together:

"Nick, you're thinking you're going to fail. Remember, these are just thoughts—not real. Imagine them as hecklers in the stands. You can't turn 'em away at the entrance. You've mastered challenges before. Go channel the strength that I know is in you."

Expect this tool to feel unnatural—because it is. But choose the short-term problem of feeling awkward rather than the long-term problem of overthinking meaningful moments.

EXTERNALIZE YOUR OVERTHINKING BY TURNING IT INTO ART

TIME: 5–10 MINUTES

This tool reconfigures ruminations or worries as less threatening and more predictable—as art to observe open-mindedly.

Transforming your unhelpful thoughts into a visual symbol can help you unhook from intense self-focus, where you fixate on symptoms, causes, meanings, or consequences of *why* you feel so bad or "future tripping" about *what* upcoming situations might mean. This change in perspective, a form of creative "cognitive defusion," allows you to curiously observe thoughts with fresh eyes—not with an agenda to judge or control. Interacting with pesky thoughts in playful or unique ways can help you gain psychological space from cycles of rumination and worry.

NOTES *Transforming your inner world into images helps you face fears and tolerate discomfort in new ways. Seeing your thoughts as pictures outside your head allows you to get comfortable in, or even bored of, their presence.*

INSTRUCTIONS

❶ Consider these questions. Don't linger too long. Go with your gut. What would your overthinking inner voice look like if it were a person or character (real or imagined)? Describe its features. Where is this figure? What action are they taking? Are they flying, sitting, pointing their finger at you?

❷ Use a free artificial intelligence text-to-image tool, like Open AI, to flesh out your imagination. Type your detailed description into the prompt box of this AI text-to-image generator. Keep revising your prompt until it feels right. Submit. Revise as many times as you want.

❸ Once you decide on an image, print it out and keep it near you. Fold it up and place it in your wallet or keep it near your working space.

❹ When you go hard into overthinking, peek at this image.

Take some deep breaths.

This is your overactive mind "externalized"—in focus, less believable, and outside of you. Get used to seeing it. Turn to it when you're in an overthinking mode. Acknowledge the picture, maybe even get bored of it, and then move on to what matters in real life.

SAY THE SCARY WORDS OUT LOUD TO DEPOWER THEM

TIME: 2 MINUTES

Do you ever notice that when you repeat a word over and over quickly, it begins to sound like gibberish? There's a term for that: "semantic satiation." Like overeating, repeating the word "satiates" your brain's processing of its meaning. One study found this repetition reduces discomfort from distressing thoughts more than attempting to control or distract from them.

Take the English word "wolf." But you might associate it with werewolves, fairy-tale characters, or those ironic T-shirts with howling wolves. It may evoke wolf packs to an Alaskan, but as a Chicagoan, I think of the Chicago Wolves pro hockey team. But none of these associations are hardwired into "wolf."

Unlike other animals, humans collect and attach endless associations, emotions, contexts, relationships, and ideas ("relational frames") to single words. This simplifies our thinking and communication. But it can also make us feel like our head's going to explode.

NOTES *This exercise is best when you're alone and have some tolerance for experimentation.*

INSTRUCTIONS

1 Set a timer for 45 seconds. Repeat "wolf" out loud as fast as possible while fully pronouncing the word.

2 What did you notice about the word *wolf*—did it become strange-sounding or lose meaning?

3 Now, let's take this a step further. The most painful, Big Bad Words of your inner voice often stem from "core beliefs," ingrained perceptions that influence how you view yourself, others, and the world.

The next time you catch yourself overthinking, try asking yourself: What are my repetitive thoughts attempting to say about me, others, or the world at a deeper level?

When you have the answer, ask yourself: *Why would this situation be so bad? What would it mean about me if this belief or thought were true or happened? Then what would happen? Then what?*

Eventually, you end up identifying beliefs that you'd be a: "failure," "not enough," "unworthy," "stupid," or "weak." These are common beliefs/words with weight that get buried beneath everyday inner chatter.

Now, find your Big Bad Words, try repeating them, and taking them off their pedestal.

TOOL ④

GET SOME PERSPECTIVE BY TIME TRAVELING

TIME: 5 MINUTES

As a human, you're a mental time traveler, so why not use your superpower for good? This imagery exercise takes the perspective of your far-in-the-future, more seasoned self—five, ten, or thirty years ahead, a technique psychologists label "temporal distancing."

Temporal distancing requires mental agility to view current experiences through the lens of an older version of you. Doing this helps redirect attention to the impermanence of your high-anxiety moments. A developing area of research finds that it can lead to feeling less down on yourself and more optimistic when facing daily stressors.

NOTES *This tool works against "projection bias," which assumes that your future self will share your current values, beliefs, and behaviors, overlooking that you will inevitably change more than you think. Just as your tastes in food, music, and politics have evolved, so will your view of passing stressful thoughts that seem to last forever.*

INSTRUCTIONS

❶ Select an event or concern from your past or present that stirs strong emotions. Or choose a moment of analysis paralysis about a decision.

❷ Take some deep, slow breaths to center yourself.

❸ Journey through time to ground yourself in the present.

One week into the future: Envision sitting where you are right now but in a week. Imagine your physical, emotional, and mental space. Contemplate how your thoughts and feelings related to this issue have changed with some distance of time. Does the intensity of your worry or fear shift? Recognize the transient quality of how you feel now. "Time heals" is a cliché for a reason.

One year, then five years ahead: Again, take some slow breaths. Envision sitting where you are right now but in one year. Then, five years. Consider changes in your passions and beliefs, new technologies, cultural changes, or shifts in your family and community. With this perspective, reimagine how your current concerns will be remembered and perhaps shrink in importance.

Thirty years ahead: Project thirty years ahead. Assume you're alive, thriving, grayer, and wise with experience. Assess the long-term significance of your current distress. What's the story you will tell about this moment? Will you even remember it?

TOOL ⑤

DISTINGUISH FACTS FROM JUDGMENTS

TIME: 5 MINUTES

This tool is all about reporting live on the scene of your overthinking mind, like an unbiased news reporter.

We all have that inner Ron Burgundy full of terrible hot takes, car chases, and overconfidence. It's easy to confuse editorials with factual reports in our high-information news environments. This tool helps you prioritize the facts instead of endless mental clickbait, distinguishing descriptive thoughts from evaluative ones. This rewires your thoughts, so they're less emotionally charged.

Descriptive (fact-based) thoughts are direct observations and are undebatable. "*That is a hat with a Chicago Bulls logo.*" Evaluative (judgment-based) thoughts are controversial, debatable, or extreme. "*That Bulls hat was only trendy in the nineties and doesn't fit your face at all.*" Our overthinking minds have a habit of confusing evaluation with description.

NOTES *This tool is also inspired by acceptance and commitment therapy (ACT), which helps people embrace their inner worlds and pursue meaningful actions.*

1. UNHELPFUL THINKING STYLES

Cognitive-behavioral therapists often refer to "unhelpful thinking styles," a concept introduced by pioneering psychologists Aaron Beck and David Burns that fuels harsh self-judgments. Do any of these ring a bell for you?

- **All-or-nothing thinking:** Viewing things in absolute, black-and-white categories.
- **Mental filter:** Focusing only on negative details and ignoring positive ones.
- **Overgeneralizing:** Drawing broad conclusions from a single event.
- **Disqualifying the positive:** Ignoring or invalidating positive experiences.
- **Jumping to conclusions:** Making negative interpretations without evidence.
- **Magnification and minimization:** Exaggerating negatives and understating positives.
- **Emotional reasoning:** Believing something is true because it *feels* true.
- **Should statements:** Placing rigid expectations on oneself or others.
- **Labeling:** Assigning global negative labels to oneself or others.
- **Personalization:** Blaming oneself for events outside personal control.

2. CABLE NEWS VS. HARD NEWS

Think of a daily routine that you have, or once had (e.g., something as simple as brushing your teeth each morning).

Cable news version: Either in your notes or in your head, provide colorful commentary and judgments about this routine, positive or negative in tone, bringing in your unhelpful thinking styles.

Hard news version: Now write down facts about your routine—the who, what, where, when. Try to notice and refrain from diving into these unhelpful thinking styles.

See the difference?

Now, recall a recent situation where your mind acted like a harsh critic. What was the cable news version of events? What was the hard news version?

GET SOME PERSPECTIVE BY EMBRACING AWE

TIME: 5–10 MINUTES

Awe is a feeling of wonder when encountering something larger than yourself. It's that moment when, lacking 20-20 vision, you first get your corrective lenses, and suddenly, the blades of grass and lettering on street signs spring into razor-sharp focus and electrifying color. Seeking out everyday ways to re-see in high definition can free you from the "whys" and "whats" of overthinking and lead you to "whoa."

A growing body of research has found that cultivating awe changes how you see the world and connects you to others. It can reduce stress, boost social connections and your immune system, and even sharpen your brain, making weak arguments less persuasive.

Awe researcher Dacher Keltner hypothesizes that awe evolved in us to defend against stress, rejection, and loneliness and documented awe's eight wonders: the cycle of life and death, "moral beauty" of courage or virtue, energizing effects of group events like rallies and concerts, nature, music, visual design, spirituality/religion, and epiphanies.

NOTES *Awe isn't just for the lucky few. You can find it in the bubbling-up anticipation before the beat drops at a concert, witnessing firefighters make rescues, seeing the Swiss Alps, or realizing a brilliant idea. If you choose, you can try to marvel at whatever surrounds you now. What collective effort built the structures of your current room?*

INSTRUCTIONS

❶ Reflect on what makes you feel alive and full of wonder.

❷ Put your phone out of sight, take some deep breaths, and turn your undivided imagination to something out your window or in your home that you appreciate or value but would normally overlook. You can play classical music to add to the drama and make the moment more emotionally moving.

What do you see? A black-and-white picture of your immigrant grandparents who came here with nothing? An impossibly built cityscape, subway entrance, grassland, farmland, mountains?

❸ Amplify potentially awe-inspiring objects of attention. Notice the fabric, configurations, and basic nature of your focus. Breathe in and out slowly. Sink into whatever you're looking at.

- Make routine moments significant: What's the backstory of what you see? What makes it unique and irreplaceable?
- Approach familiar sights and sensations with "not-knowing" eyes: What would amaze you if you were experiencing this for the very first time?
- Consider the context or history: How tall was that familiar oak tree when that nearby house was built decades ago?
- Appreciate the potential story or craft behind everyday experiences: What were some of the best jokes from that night of stand-up?

❹ Document *after* you've soaked it in: Don't be quick to move on. Create a dedicated section in your notes called "Awe." Record your awe experiences and revisit them when your life is humming *or* hard-hitting.

———

This exercise is inspired by Jonah Paquette's Awestruck, *2020.*

CHAPTER FIVE

Common Overthinking Scenarios

In theory, there is no difference between theory and practice. In practice, there is.

—Yogi Berra

O verthinking ambushes you with worry just before you step up to the plate. It can torment you with nervousness for days or twist you into pretzels of indecision. It can look like slow-burning regret that lasts years or rapid-fire thoughts aimed inward at self-worth or outward at rivals. Some days, overthinking is vague, covering everything and solving nothing.

Living in your head keeps you from stepping into the stadium and putting this inner tormentor to the test. This chapter does that, putting these tools to work in real-world scenarios. However, if you want help now, check out the cheat sheet on page 131.

No "perfect" way to apply these methods exists, so keep experimenting. Each scenario is a composite drawn from men I've worked with in clinical settings, friends, and family, with privacy preserved through altered details, settings, and names.

DECIDING BETWEEN TWO REASONABLE OPTIONS

After years of swiping on dating apps and a nagging sense that *maybe there's someone even better just around the corner*, James lands on a promising match.

He mentally fast-forwards and envisions how her hospitable, Southern upbringing could jive with his Long Island gruff. In a flash, he rewinds to a previous date that held promise but ended in an awkward mismatch. This disappointing flashback crushes James's spirit, leaving him questioning: *What am I missing?*

It's been a few days since they matched, and James senses pressure to initiate or miss an opportunity. But deciding on an opening gambit is risky: directness can seem desperate, returning him to the conveyor belt of male dating profiles, but too much charm triggers an "ick." Cut to the chase, or build up the romantic plot and play harder to get? Each seems reasonable, keeping him in decision paralysis.

James delays. He types a message, edits, and deletes. A half hour passes. His brain simulates outcomes based on memories of past dating near-misses and fizzle-outs. It fills in gaps, integrating data from her profile picture, job title, and education. Layer this with a tightrope walk: balancing expectations of take-charge masculinity while steering clear of old-school power dynamics and cringy pickup artistry.

Online dating data reveals a disparity: while women report feeling overwhelmed by the high volume of messages they receive (54 percent say they feel this way), men often struggle with a lack of responses, leaving 64 percent feeling insecure. This mismatch can disappoint users on either side, leading them to abandon dating platforms. But James isn't giving up. Overthinking is a symptom of deeply caring. His heart thumps and jaw clenches, sending signals back to his brain, influencing his perception that this choice is super high stakes.

STOP OVERTHINKING IN ITS TRACKS

When deciding between two reasonable options, get up and get out before making any hot-headed decisions. Tap into your go-to list of actions from **Catch Your Overthinking and Break the Cycle with Movement** (page 24). This helps you acknowledge your state of mind nonjudgmentally and then pivot to body movement that switches up your setting, allowing your brain to reset. Yet, a nagging thought might hold you back: *going outside during a time crunch is unproductive.* Changing your scenery, moving your body, walking, running, or strength training is more directly productive than chasing your tail.

Remember, emotions can help you decide. If you're just feeling "stuck," you might remain in decision paralysis. Try to track first what's going on in your body (e.g., areas of tension) as a lead-in to getting specific with **Decode Your Emotions to Find the Best Solution** (page 28). Maybe you label yourself with "nervous apprehension, which makes you cautious about getting hurt yet hopeful." When you name, you tame. Specific emotion words bring order to emotional storms, grounding you and calming the inner chaos. Armed with more nuanced emotions perhaps allows you to own your healthy nervousness and hopefulness in ways you hadn't.

Worried thoughts can be like bullshitters at a bar. Core values, though—what you care about and how you want to live—are straight shooters. Tap into your wise inner navigator by trying the **Know What You Value** tool (page 77). Maybe your decision narrows down: Which choice brings you closer to finding a romantic partner who adds smarts and stability and shares in your life?

Perhaps you may send a message driven by hope rather than fear, striking a balance between charm and sincerity.

Only you can decide.

Take a look at the Decision-Making Cheat Sheet on page 131 for more insight into outsmarting analysis paralysis in other sorts of decisions.

BROTHERHOOD LOST: DWELLING ON PAST (IN)ACTIONS

Over the years, Mark and Jeff's thick-as-thieves friendship grew distant. Marriage, kids, and thousands of miles of distance didn't help. Their boyhood forging rivalries outdoors in large groups, their adrenaline-driven adventures, and unmatched closeness after competition seemed long in the past.

How do you even make new guy friends without that special sauce of shared memories, with no established inside language, jokes, or banter? Sometimes, if you miss out on knowing the knuckleheaded teenage boy that lurks within a man, you don't see pivotal parts of his character.

Mark, approaching middle age, squints back to those days and cannot shake his guilt about Jeff. After diving head-on into his relationship with his wife, Mark had stopped calling him back, taking it for granted that he'd be waiting in the wings when needed. He couldn't muster energy. "Didn't have time."

The deep emotional ties of boyhood friendships die off as they approach adulthood. Now, more than ever, Mark is not alone in feeling isolated: Between 2003 and

2022, American men's average face-to-face socializing time decreased by nearly 30 percent.

As years pass, it's natural for your friend count to dwindle. But as isolation sets in, Mark's mind grows ruminative, focusing on how bad a friend he's been and how he relies on his wife for a social life. Friendships aren't meant to be stored away on an as-needed basis.

STOP OVERTHINKING IN ITS TRACKS

While the decision to call Jeff to reconnect seems simple, Mark dreads it, knowing he'd gone MIA and is full of rationales about why he shouldn't reach out.

Taking a beat and categorizing overthinking can be helpful. Mark's situation fits under the heading of rumination—dwelling on regrets. Building awareness by categorizing overthinking using **Map Your Routes and Exits** (page 34) is called "metacognition" and refers to thinking about your type of thinking. It can help you build awareness and move your thinking from passive and vague to more concrete and action-oriented. This can make space for gratitude for what you have—that each of you is thriving separately. Friendships approaching middle age might look different yet remain valuable—maybe more distant, less alcohol-infused and high-flying, but more honest.

Rumination also signals a moment to tune into your emotions for guidance—like sheet music. Emotions are information cues, directing you to methods of coping and communication. This is crucial to practice continually. Again, turn to your tool **Decode Your Emotions to Find the Best Solution** (page 28). Dig deeper than just "upset." Own your sadness-regret-relief and notice where this shows up in your body. Sometimes, yes, there's a relief from rationalizing why you can't reach out. Own that relief because emotions can be contradictory. Emotions are messy data worth sorting through, not inherently "good" or "bad."

Ask yourself: *What do my emotions signal about what I need to do—not want to do?*

Sometimes, this means countering over-learned habits and impulses head-on. Psychologists call this "opposite action"; for example, if unpleasant emotions motivate you to lean away, notice that impulse . . . and then do the opposite: lean *in* with a long-lost pal. Resurrect the friendship to adapt to who you are today.

WHAT WILL BE MY WORTH? WORRYING ABOUT FUTURE EVENTS

If Sanjay's compensation is low this year, it's not a bummer; it's a crushing defeat.

Early December rings in worry season, as Sanjay's income stems from end-of-year compensation. It's a "slow economy," but in the last 10 years of working in sales, it's consistently been a period that launches him into anxiety. Sanjay hasn't found words to accurately capture the bone-deep mix of dread with a tinge of hopefulness. He bites his tongue, careful about "burdening" his free-spirited husband or stressing his immigrant parents with his "spoiled" neediness.

Sanjay's stomach sinks when he sees his boss turning the corner. He imagines downsizing his lifestyle and his husband's look of disappointment.

With layoffs lurking, the question gnaws as he stares at the ceiling, attempting to sleep: *What'll be my worth this year?*

The months-long anticipation during the start of East Coast winters (overthinking cue) triggers anxiety (an urge to *know*, to resolve ambiguity). The craving for relief prompts Sanjay's mental ritual of worrying—which helps distract him from feelings of fear and shame about the possibility of failing as a provider. This loop cranks up the volume of his mind each year, increasing the cumulative damage of long-term stress.

STOP OVERTHINKING IN ITS TRACKS

When you know that certain times of the year bring about elevations in toxic stress, utilize **Check In with Your Stress** (page 44). This allows you to anticipate stress spikes and preemptively prioritize sleep consistency, exercise, diet, and social health interventions. For data-driven guys like Sanjay, "numbers don't lie." **Add Up the Time You Spend Overthinking** (page 66) can help you track the impact of overthinking—and the time you spend attempting to distract from spiraling thoughts. It helps target your overthinking pain points—where and when you overthink.

But amid high anxiety, make it a daily practice to ground yourself in the present moment to reduce your physiological arousal. Slow things down in your body. Notice your feet anchored to the ground. Use an evidence-based breathing technique like the **"cyclic sigh"** (page 22) or a **brief body scan** (page 23) from chapter one. Harness the power of music using **Listen Closely to the Bassist** (page 32). This "focused mindfulness" activity is the art and science of returning to one thing, like your breath—or an overlooked instrument like the bass. It focuses your divided attention and settles jumpy emotions. One famous 2009 study demonstrated that music helped calm presurgery patients, serving as an alternative to medications.

You can also use another method that helps you practice raising your stress tolerance. The tool **Raise Your Stress Tolerance by Expanding Your Visual Field** (page 56) widens your visual field during a "fight-or-flight" body response. When you feel your heart thumping rapidly, try to practice taking a more panoramic view as it pairs inner body stress with outward calm. It can make you grittier and more resilient over time and with practice.

LEAD-UP TO A BIG MOMENT: LAST-MINUTE, HIGH-STRESS PERFECTIONISM

The blinking cursor on Caleb's laptop screen taunts him, and the dull ache in his neck seems like a tightening metal clamp. It's 1:00 a.m., and he's been feverishly tinkering on PowerPoint for hours, hitting a wall as he prepares for tomorrow's presentation to his manager.

Caleb has worked on this project for months. The potential is exciting but so is the burden of responsibility. He's worked on developing his code in a constant state of what psychologists call "reasonable mind," prioritizing logic. But a cold, rational approach (much like the opposite but fiery "emotion mind") backfires when overused.

Caleb is stuck running mental simulations. His over-carefulness keeps him self-doubting. Time's running out.

Despite understanding this project better than anyone and being well-prepared to explain it, he expects harsh judgment from his boss. So he delays, waiting for the perfect words to make his boss's criticism impossible.

Perfectionism may begin with healthy, high personal standards but transitions into believing *others*, such as a boss, expect flawlessness. Caleb has crossed the border from pursuing excellence into the war zone of excessive self-criticism and chasing shadows. His self-worth is overly reliant on achievements.

Perfectionism goes into overdrive with procrastination—an irrational delay of behavior. Perfectionism is avoiding future unpleasant emotions such as fear or boredom: Caleb justifies delaying and starting a task at the eleventh hour by setting unreachable standards and obsessing over details.

Caleb constantly delays things to protect himself against the fear of his boss's harsh criticism and humiliation. This, in the end, only fills him with more regret, anxiety, and inadequacy.

STOP OVERTHINKING IN ITS TRACKS

Sometimes, it's hard to know if you're constructively thinking or unconstructively spinning your wheels with "unhelpful thinking styles." Use **Distinguish Facts from Judgments** (page 94) to rein in your thinking frenzy. Like an unbiased reporter, this activity gives you a quick perspective by translating your mind's conspiracies into facts. Try *hand*writing this on a piece of paper. It's more personalized and gets you out of your head.

Tap into your mindfulness and breathing exercises. Zoom out from "catastrophizing" beliefs with the exercise

Get Some Perspective by Time Traveling (page 92). This mental imagery method helps you view intense, immediate concerns from the perspective of your future, wiser self. This fosters a more balanced, long-term mindset.

The tool **Be Your Own Elite Coach** (page 86) is also a practical technique for handling stress and leading up to a big event. Research on self-talk finds that silently self-coaching using your name and "you" rather than "I" helps interpret anxieties as challenges and calms high emotions. Pair this with **Transform Pressure into Better Performance** (page 51). This method, used by elite athletes, involves rethinking your anxiety as excitement and a challenge, which is useful right before going on the big stage. Reinterpreting a racing heart as helpful adrenaline and jitters as necessary pregame energy shifts performance anxiety into a motivator. It pumps you up to perform as opposed to nitpick and delay.

DROWNING IN CONFUSING TEARS: NAVIGATING RELATIONSHIP ISSUES

Greg's girlfriend has grown frustrated, and understandably so. She's expressed her desire for marriage, but he's not ready for that leap. Under pressure, he loses his voice. When he wants to communicate his love, it's like a frustrating logjam between his internal world and outward expression.

When his girlfriend brings up marriage with the best intentions, Greg, out of habit and self-protection, repeats what he believes she wants to hear—*yes, it'll happen*. After this, Greg withdraws, opting for the quiet of disengagement over the chaos of confrontation. He fears that any attempt to communicate might only deepen their rift, leaving him feeling even more like a failure.

Greg ruminates on his girlfriend's frequent tears during these marriage talks. He interprets her crying as overpowering emotional persuasion that clears the deck of his needs. From his vantage, tears are overwhelming and seem unproductive to connection. Yet, his girlfriend isn't in any way purposely using her tears to persuade him; her crying is a natural response, an authentic expression of her feelings to reach a mutual understanding.

Later, sleepless that night, Greg fumes at how her tears instantly transform him into the bad guy and overshadow his real marriage reservations. His anger rebounds inward: her unhappiness is suddenly translated to: *I'm underperforming—falling short of "being enough." Why do I always fail to make it right?*

Greg's style of overthinking centers on rumination, which research finds can branch into brooding or reflective pondering. Brooding focuses on unpleasant feelings without solutions ("Why?"), whereas reflection can elicit deeper understanding or solutions ("What now?").

From the outside, Greg's brooding and powerlessness propels him to exert power in other ways, like driving wildly fast on the freeway. His girlfriend doesn't know about his brooding, just his "high alcohol tolerance," and retreats to multiplayer video games—a stimulating, yet mind-numbing, getaway.

STOP OVERTHINKING IN ITS TRACKS

Men are commonly told to "open up" but this well-intended suggestion doesn't instantly reverse decades-long instincts to squash emotions. Another powerful way to work on rumination and sharpen the skill of vulnerable expression is through stream-of-consciousness writing. Even if writing seems like a pain in the ass, it's a powerful way to dislodge deeper insights. The tool **Protect Your Wake-Up Time** (page 54) is described as a morning activity, but it can also be used throughout the day.

Self-reliance is a virtue until it begins to block progress.

Ask yourself: *What is the worst that could happen if the bad outcome I imagine did occur? What would this outcome say about me?*

Write about that for a few minutes.

The crux of many men's inner relationship roadblocks stems from the (perceived) failed mission to be indispensable, to strive toward a bigger purpose, and to *matter*. Falling short and feeling as if you're burdening others hurts. It's easy to blame others or yourself. But mattering doesn't have to happen only in romantic relationships. Live an action-oriented existence outside your romantic life: try the exercise **Help Someone Else to De-Stress Yourself** (page 59). Research finds that giving back to others when stressed can even lower your blood pressure. It helps you mine untapped empathy and build camaraderie.

How can you use your unique skills—such as a green thumb, tidying up logistical nightmares, or cooking—to help a neighbor, overworked coworker, family member, friend, or maybe someone you've lost touch with?

CRUMBLING UNDER PROVIDER ANXIETY: FINANCIAL DECISION-MAKING

His boyhood buddies nicknamed him The Rock, a nod to his pro-wrestler-looking physique. Fast-forward decades later, and with mounting financial worries, Roy secretly feels his badass persona is a facade.

Roy's mind seizes on the quiet of the night, and he transforms into The Count—inspecting his checking accounts, refreshing his banking mobile app, running the numbers, and revving the engines of his adrenaline and cortisol.

Working in finance was a liberation from Roy's childhood financial adversities. As he ascended his bank's ranks, he and his girlfriend agreed to wait on a wedding, but then unexpectedly got pregnant. They decided she'd be the lead parent covering the home front when their son was born, pausing her professional ambitions. This cornered him into the role of their family's chief financial officer. At first, this seemed like a sacred duty, one he was cut out for . . . until predicaments arose—a newborn and sleepless nights, the pull between the demanding home front and dominating work front.

The more Roy handled the stressful family finances, the more his girlfriend stepped back, fortifying the home front he'd vacated.

Roy can't take his mind off the possibility of financial ruin. He keeps quiet about not really having it all together, as opening that up would mean challenging the unspoken agreement of their family roles. He knows his girlfriend has set aside her promising career and struggles under the weight of her own immense parenting responsibilities. Revealing any cracks might make The Rock unlovable.

But from the outside, everyone sees a self-reliant company man who's always just "all right," "all good," "okay."

STOP OVERTHINKING IN ITS TRACKS

In this situation, Roy benefits from gaining confidence in asking for help using a tool like **Prevent Stress by Skillfully Asking for Help** (page 61). Money, like sex, often carries shame. Many men feel they *should* know how it works and avoid asking for directions for fear of seeming indecisive, weak, or naïve. Financial guidance can help you see how super-convincing catastrophic beliefs actually misalign with reality. Asking work colleagues how they handle work-life flow or money management normalizes the struggles of modern fatherhood.

In real life, cold calculus and accounting are vital to financial health. But with family financial decision-making, you can also interpret money as a metaphor for flexibility, love, or nurturing your family's dreams. As crucial as seeking professional financial guidance is knowing how you'd *spend* your hard-earned resources. The combination of **Know What You Value** (page 77) and **Settle Your Mind with Meaningful Goals** (page 81) can help translate fixations on finances into something more profound, concrete, and inspiring than just external rewards.

Maybe you care about *carefully and thoughtfully managing money, so you have resources to spend on memorable experiences with your family (because you didn't as a kid)*. Maybe that's your "why."

Carrying the financial burden and faltering can boomerang and strike you in the heart with beliefs about "failure."

But what's in the word "fail"?

Humans take their minds *so* seriously. Take away the unhealthy emotional charge of certain haunting words with **Say the Scary Words Out Loud to Depower Them** (page 90). It's a playful solution that can transform harsh self-talk into silly sounds. Learning to be playful is perhaps the most underrated tool to combat those snarling core beliefs—like the word "fail."

MANAGING PERSONAL APPEARANCE AND SELF-IMAGE

Like many men, Raymond has taken hair loss hard. But he keeps a stiff upper lip.

Looking in the mirror, he's forced to face his insecurities. This seems especially important on days like today, when he's preparing for his 10-year high school reunion. He catastrophizes: What if old pals don't even recognize him? What if classmates gossip about his baldness? He flashes to the ruthless halls of his high school.

Raymond's hair loss has become a fixation—evidence of falling short of expectations and self-assuredness. Hair loss can lead to significant psychological distress, including anxiety, depression, decreased confidence, and social phobia that's not easy for many men to adjust to.

From a clinical psychologist's perspective, a hyperfocus on thinning hair—or other perceived body imperfections—can be a surface obsession detracting from deeper, intolerable feelings; in Raymond's case, unresolved estrangements and loss.

Raymond had lost touch with his younger athletic identity—a gut punch of sadness, regret, and anxiety whenever a skinnier, more muscular image of him popped up on an iPhone slideshow from years past.

Despite spending money on hair-regrowing efforts, nothing has worked. But he does have some power to reengage with *controllable* aspects of his health—for example, eating healthier and restarting his morning runs with his dog. Appearance fixations or cosmetic overthinking about male pattern baldness (despite occurring in most men during their lifetime) can deflect from less tangible, deeper-seated desires.

STOP OVERTHINKING IN ITS TRACKS

Nitpicking about hair follicles neglects the vast, lush landscape surrounding you and your opportunities for meaningful self-growth.

Raymond's attention to time-consumingly combing his thinning hair covers up his unmet but profound desire to belong and feel competent. Understanding this about yourself can be a practical pivot from constant faultfinding.

In the mirror, ask yourself: *What do I really need deep down?* Be honest.

When you label your emotions and get to know the hidden longings within them, you can problem-solve to better satisfy them. Use the **Uncover Your Deeper**

Drives to Find Clarity (page 39) tool that syncs up with unmet drives. For instance, hair loss might alert you to a drive to belong (social acceptance) or to grow more competent (be sturdy and strong). But there are more viable paths to each.

Sometimes, it can be helpful to pivot from bodily insecurities and remind yourself that your body can tackle challenges with resilience. But you may have to "stack" resistance training or other forms of exercise into your schedule.

One way to weave something vital like exercise into a busy schedule is to hitch it to existing, well-established routines using **Stack Your Habits to Think Less, Do More** (page 75). Build belonging and competence into everyday behaviors. Here's just one example:

CHOOSE CHALLENGE OVER CONVENIENCE

- *Cue*: As you enter school or work, see the stairs as an arena to help restore a more youthful version of yourself.
- *Habit*: Skip steps and move quickly (yes, even if you're tired). It's a physical challenge and a daily commitment to health. Build upon it.
- *Reward*: Reach the top feeling physically activated.

WHAT SHOULD I DO IN LIFE? OVERTHINKING PURPOSE

Approaching his mid-fifties, Ed, recently divorced and new to his neighborhood, is at a crossroads.

Navigating the rocky terrain of single fatherhood, he struggles to find his voice in close-knit dad circles. He feels like an interloper on the WhatsApp group chats he's been invited to—lifelines for carpools and parenting hacks. The assumption that he has a spouse in the wings only reinforces his "outsider" status, a self-belief that's hung around from a childhood of moving between military bases.

Ed's finally out of the little kid stage of parenting. He imagines pursuing his dream of being an addiction counselor. Leaving his job to begin school, even part time, seems impossible or, depending on his mood, within reach. His values are crystal clear, and his aspiration to guide others in their sobriety is heartfelt—born of firsthand battles with addiction.

But Ed easily gets lost in what psychologists label "self-referential" thinking—unfocused worries/ruminations and unease in assessing and contemplating your identity or how you fit into the world. When Ed needs to concentrate at work, he drifts—imagines his large, middle-aged frame squeezed into a classroom desk, standing out among all the fresh-faced twentysomethings.

A Harvard University study in 2010 revealed how the human mind wanders from activities about 47 percent of waking hours. Mind-wandering (even on pleasant topics) can promote creativity or be a winding path to unhappiness. Learning to stay present and focused during these moments boosts your well-being.

STOP OVERTHINKING IN ITS TRACKS

If you are in touch with what matters to you (values), like Ed, you need clear, achievable aims—a reliable compass. Go hard into goal setting with **Settle Your Mind with Meaningful Goals** (page 81). This activity enables you to progress in manageable, small steps, saving time from getting lost in mind meanderings.

Mind-wandering often operates below awareness, and a variety of short mindful awareness exercises can help. There are countless apps to choose from, or you can utilize your calming tools from chapter one.

But how do you adequately squeeze present-moment awareness into your day?

An open-ended calendar is a recipe for mind wandering. While the time management tool **Block Out Time for Tasks That Matter to You** (page 69) may seem effortful, it can have a lasting impact. It involves setting aside specific blocks for forgettable but self-fortifying activities, like breathing exercises, body scans, or focused attention mindfulness. Blocking out rituals for mundane meal planning or administrative work also conserves mental energy.

When you finally have some clear direction on where you want to go, cultivating awe is a powerful practice to return you to where you are in the present. Use **Get Some Perspective by Embracing Awe** (page 97) to activate wonder and curiosity and transform awesome everyday experiences into higher definition.

Try recording your awe experiences for one whole day. But do it only *after* you've fully taken in and amplified what you're focusing on—city buildings that are architectural feats or your kid's innocent creativity as they play with Magna-Tiles.

Put away your phone until you need it. We scramble to capture, share, and preserve big moments in modern life, clutching our devices and trading in the here and now, overlooking the purpose hiding in plain sight before our eyes.

Overthinking robs you of the precious present moment. Cultivating awe recoups that loss.

Conclusion

You've made it to the end, and that's an achievement. It's not lost on me that this is hard. I've asked you to rebel against your mind's deeply grooved settings that bully you with threats, attempt perfection, and dwell on regrets. I've asked you to meet your mind in all its vastness.

But you are better equipped with fresh self-insight. You now have methods to stay present, find calm, manage stress, reclaim lost productivity, and gain breathing room when your inner voice becomes too much. Don't forget to tap into the handouts in the appendix to help you get oriented on which methods to use and when.

The blob inside your skull was designed as a threat detector that operates under unstable conditions with incomplete information. Overthinking is a result of this essential brain feature gone rogue. So keep at it. Try working on these new moves in the low-stakes practice fields of ordinary moments, not in the sold-out coliseum during peak stress. Practice when you're in an open, motivated mood.

Remember: clumsiness leads to comfort, new habits, and rewiring—eventually, a quieter mind that frees you to charge forward.

You got this.

Appendix

When to Utilize Your Tools

DAILY

- Calm Down Quicker with the "Cyclic Sigh" (page 22)
- Catch Your Overthinking and Break the Cycle with Movement (page 24)
- Decode Your Emotions to Find the Best Solution (page 28)
- Map Your Routes and Exits (page 34)
- Protect Your Wake-Up Time (page 54)
- Block Out Time for Tasks That Matter to You (page 69)
- Distinguish Facts from Judgments (page 94)
- Get Some Perspective by Embracing Awe (page 97)

REGULARLY: MONTHLY, ALTERNATING MONTHS, OR QUARTERLY

- Check In with Your Stress (page 44)
- Add Up the Time You Spend Overthinking (page 66)
- Know What You Value (page 77)
- Settle Your Mind with Meaningful Goals (page 81)

CIRCUMSTANTIAL

IN-THE-MOMENT

- Map Your Routes and Exits (page 34)
- Uncover Your Deeper Drives to Find Clarity (page 39)
- Distinguish Facts from Judgments (page 94)
- Listen Closely to the Bassist (page 32)
- Transform Pressure into Better Performance (page 51)
- Prevent Stress by Skillfully Asking for Help (page 61)
- Be Your Own Elite Coach (page 86)

SCHEDULED

- Block Out Time for Tasks That Matter to You (page 69)
- Protect Your Wake-Up Time (page 54)
- Settle Your Mind with Meaningful Goals (page 81)
- Stack Your Habits to Think Less, Do More (page 75)

PREVENTIVE

- Check In with Your Stress (page 44)
- Add Up the Time You Spend Overthinking (page 66)
- Know What You Value (page 77)
- Raise Your Stress Tolerance by Expanding Your Visual Field (page 56)
- Help Someone Else to De-Stress Yourself (page 59)

- Replace Bedtime Overthinking with "Constructive Worry" (page 72)
- Say the Scary Words Out Loud to Depower Them (page 90)

REFLECTIVE

- Decode Your Emotions to Find the Best Solution (page 28)
- Get Some Perspective by Embracing Awe (page 97)
- Uncover Your Deeper Drives to Find Clarity (page 39)
- Externalize Your Overthinking by Turning It into Art (page 88)

Decision-Making Cheat Sheet

OUTSMART ANALYSIS PARALYSIS

Follow these steps sequentially or move between them as needed to outsmart the tyranny of indecision. Refer to relevant tools from the book.

---

❶ Is Your Decision Pivotal or Trivial?

Will this decision potentially improve your well-being or add more meaning and fulfillment to your life in *one week*? How about in *one year*?

YES: Proceed to step two.

NO: Classify as "Trivial." Decide quickly. You've just freed up time to devote to something that lights you up.

(Continues on next page)

❷ Evaluate Decision Commitment

Assess the permanence of your choices:

HIGH COMMITMENT: e.g., 30-year mortgage, non-refundable airfare.

    If High Commitment: Set aside time to decide. Proceed to step three.

LOW COMMITMENT: e.g., Short-term rental, refundable airfare.

    If Low Commitment or options seem very similar, decide quicker and anticipate "outcome bias"—when you unfairly judge a decision by the *result* rather than how sensible it was at the time. If both options differ slightly, chances are they have similar risks of going wrong. Hindsight's 20-20! Proceed to step three, optional.

❸ Lay Out Your Cards & Keep Boundaries

Jot down your choices and their different consequences in columns.

Set a timer: Give yourself a set amount of time to continue weighing your options.

If you're still stuck, block out a later time to continue. This reduces decision fatigue. Resume later at step four.

➠   Tool: Block Out Time for Tasks That Matter to You

❹ Gather More Data from Emotions

Are you moving *away* from regret, failure, or rejection instead of toward something you really care about (values)?

Label your emotions. What are their hidden messages? What are they motivating you to do? With this data, what do you *need* to do (not what you *want* to do)?

➠ Tool: Decode Your Emotions to Find the Best Solution

❺ Seek Advice

Consult with others you trust to gain different perspectives.

Hold on to these potentially differing viewpoints for step seven.

➠ Tool: Prevent Stress by Skillfully Asking for Help

(Continues on next page)

❻ Consult Your Future Self

Ask your future self: What advice would a future wiser *you* offer?

What might you say to a friend in your same predicament?

➠ Tool: Get Some Perspective by Time Traveling

❼ Check Alignment with Values

Lay out your choices again with these various outlooks and insights from trusted others, your "future self," and what you might say to a friend in a similar situation.

Which of the options are most in harmony with your true, freely chosen values—not just comparatively—based on external motivations, family or societal pressures, or material rewards?

➠ Tools: Uncover Your Deeper Drives to Find Clarity, Know What You Value

❽ Take a Lap, Then Decide

If overwhelmed, pause, engage in physical activity, and return to the choice. Sleep on it. You've tried to get it right.

If you still can't decide, which choice is most aligned with a long-term, aspirational goal (rather than immediate comfort)?

Embrace "good enough," and commit.

➠ Tools: Calm Down Quicker with the "Cyclic Sigh," Catch Your Overthinking and Break the Cycle with Movement, Settle Your Mind with Meaningful Goals

Resources

Atomic Habits: An Easy & Proven Way to Build Good Habits & Break Bad Ones by James Clear

Breath: The New Science of a Lost Art by James Nestor

Chatter: The Voice in Our Head by Ethan Kross

Deep Secrets: Boys' Friendships and the Crisis of Connection by Niobe Way

How Emotions Are Made: The Secret Life of the Brain by Lisa Feldman Barrett, PhD

How to Decide: Simple Tools for Making Better Choices by Annie Duke

I Don't Want to Talk About It: Overcoming the Secret Legacy of Male Depression by Terrence Real

Mindfulness by Ellen Langer

Of Boys and Men: Why the Modern Male Is Struggling, Why It Matters, and What to Do about It by Richard Reeves

Resilience: The Science of Mastering Life's Greatest Challenges by Steven M. Southwick, Dennis S. Charney, and Jonathan M. DePierro

Stress Resets: How to Soothe Your Body and Mind in Minutes by Jennifer L. Taitz, PsyD

The Algebra of Happiness: Notes on the Pursuit of Success, Love, and Meaning by Scott Galloway

The Confident Mind: A Battle-Tested Guide to Unshakable Performance by Nate Zinsser, PhD

The Liberated Mind: How to Pivot Toward What Matters by Stephen Hayes, PhD

The Male Brain by Louann Brizendine

The Will to Change by bell hooks

Under Saturn's Shadow by James Hollis

Unwinding Anxiety: New Science Shows How to Break the Cycles of Worry and Fear to Heal Your Mind by Judson Brewer, MD, PhD

References

Introduction

Acuff, J. 2021. *Soundtracks*. Baker Books.

APA.org. "Stress in America 2023." 2023. apa.org/news/press /releases/stress/2023/collective-trauma-recovery.

Augner, C., Vlasak, T., Aichhorn, W., and Barth, A. 2023. "The Association between Problematic Smartphone Use and Symptoms of Anxiety and Depression: A Meta-Analysis." *Journal of Public Health* (Oxford, England), 45 (1): 193–201. doi.org/10.1093 /pubmed/fdab350.

Brewer, J. 2021. *Unwinding Anxiety: New Science Shows How to Break the Cycles of Worry and Fear to Heal Your Mind*. Penguin Random House.

Brosschot, J. F., Gerin, W., and Thayer, J. F. 2006. "The Perseverative Cognition Hypothesis: A Review of Worry, Prolonged Stress-Related Physiological Activation, and Health." *Journal of Psychosomatic Research* 60: 113–124.

Centers for Disease Control and Prevention. 2023. "Suicide Data and Statistics." cdc.gov/suicide/suicide-data-statistics.html.

Demnitz-King, H., Göehre, I., and Marchant, N. L. 2021. "The Neuroanatomical Correlates of Repetitive Negative Thinking: A Systematic Review." *Psychiatry Research: Neuroimaging*.

Kowalski, J., Wypych, M., Marchewka, A., and Dragan, M. 2019. "Neural Correlates of Cognitive-Attentional Syndrome: An fMRI Study on Repetitive Negative Thinking Induction and Resting State Functional Connectivity." *Frontiers in Psychology* 10. doi.org/10.3389/fpsyg.2019.00648.

Krahé, C., Whyte, J., Bridge, L., Loizou, S., and Hirsch, C. R. 2019. "Are Different Forms of Repetitive Negative Thinking Associated with Interpretation Bias in Generalized Anxiety Disorder and Depression?" *Clinical Psychological Science* 7 (5): 969–981. doi.org/10.1177/2167702619851808.

Nolen-Hoeksema, S. 2016. *Women Who Think Too Much*. Hachette UK.

Solé-Padullés, C., Cattaneo, G., Marchant, N. L., María Cabello-Toscano, Lídia Mulet-Pons, Solana, J., Núria Bargalló, Tormos, J., Álvaro Pascual-Leone, and Bartrés-Faz, D. 2022. "Associations between Repetitive Negative Thinking and Resting-State Network Segregation among Healthy Middle-Aged Adults." *Frontiers in Aging Neuroscience* 14. doi.org/10.3389/fnagi.2022.1062887.

Vaish, A., Grossmann, T., and Woodward, A. 2008. "Not All Emotions Are Created Equal: The Negativity Bias in Social-Emotional Development." *Psychological Bulletin* 134 (3): 383–403. doi.org/10.1037/0033-2909.134.3.383.

van Oort, J., Tendolkar, I., Collard, R., Geurts, D. E. M., Vrijsen, J. N., Duyser, F. A., Kohn, N., Fernández, G., Schene, A. H., and van Eijndhoven, P. F. P. 2022. "Neural Correlates of Repetitive Negative Thinking: Dimensional Evidence across the Psychopathological Continuum." *Frontiers in Psychiatry* 13. doi.org/10.3389/fpsyt.2022.915316.

Chapter One

Balban, M. Y., Neri, E., Kogon, M. M., Weed, L., Nouriani, B., Jo, B., . . . and Huberman, A. D. 2023. "Brief Structured Respiration Practices Enhance Mood and Reduce Physiological Arousal." *Cell Reports Medicine* 4 (1).

Barrett, L. F. 2017. *How Emotions Are Made: The Secret Life of the Brain*. Houghton Mifflin Harcourt.

Bernstein, E. E., and McNally, R. J. 2018. "Exercise as a Buffer against Difficulties with Emotion Regulation: A Pathway to Emotional Wellbeing." *Behaviour Research and Therapy* 109: 29–36. doi.org/10.1016/j.brat.2018.07.010.

Boggio, P., Giglio, A., Nakao, C., Wingenbach, T., Marques, L., Koller, S., and Gruber, J. 2020. "Writing about Gratitude Increases Emotion-Regulation Efficacy." *The Journal of Positive Psychology* 15, 783–794. doi.org/10.1080/17439760.2019.1651893.

Bransford, J. D., and Stein, B. S. 1993. *The Ideal Problem Solver.* Centers for Teaching Excellence—Book Library, 46. digitalcommons.georgiasouthern.edu/ct2-library/46.

Cregg, D. R., and Cheavens, J. S. 2022. "Healing through Helping: An Experimental Investigation of Kindness, Social Activities, and Reappraisal as Well-Being Interventions." *The Journal of Positive Psychology.* DOI: 10.1080/17439760.2022.2154695.

Gordon, B. R., McDowell, C. P., Hallgren, M., Meyer, J. D., Lyons, M., and Herring, M. P. 2018. "Association of Efficacy of Resistance Exercise Training with Depressive Symptoms: Meta-Analysis and Meta-Regression Analysis of Randomized Clinical Trials." *JAMA Psychiatry* 75 (6): 566–576. doi.org/10.1001/jamapsychiatry.2018.0572.

Gordon, B. R., McDowell, C. P., Lyons, M., and Herring, M. P. 2017. "The Effects of Resistance Exercise Training on Anxiety: A Meta-Analysis and Meta-Regression Analysis of Randomized Controlled Trials." *Sports Medicine* (Auckland, NZ) 47 (12): 2521–2532. doi.org/10.1007/s40279-017-0769-0.

Graham, R. 2010. "A Cognitive-Attentional Perspective on the Psychological Benefits of Listening." *Music and Medicine* 2, 167–173. doi.org/10.1177/1943862110372522.

Harvard Health. "Exercise Can Boost Your Memory and Thinking Skills." October 20, 2023. Harvard Health. health.harvard.edu/mind-and-mood/exercise-can-boost-your-memory-and-thinking-skills.

Hayes S. C. 2020. "Constructing a Liberated and Modern Mind: Six Pathways from Pathology to Euthymia." *World Psychiatry: Official Journal of the World Psychiatric Association (WPA)* 19 (1): 51–52. doi.org/10.1002/wps.20715.

Kabat-Zinn, J. 2003. "Mindfulness-Based Interventions in Context: Past, Present, and Future." *Clinical Psychology: Science and Practice* 10 (2): 144–156. doi.org/10.1093/clipsy.bpg016.

Kashdan, T. B., Ferssizidis, P., Collins, R. L., and Muraven, M. 2010. "Emotion Differentiation as Resilience against Excessive Alcohol Use: An Ecological Momentary Assessment in Underage Social Drinkers." *Psychological Science* 21 (9): 1341–1347. doi.org/10.1177/0956797610379863.

Layous, K., Kumar, S. A., Arendtson, M., and Najera, A. 2023. "The Effects of Rumination, Distraction, and Gratitude on Positive and Negative Affect." *Journal of Personality and Social Psychology* 124 (5): 1053–1078. doi.org/10.1037/pspp0000440.

Lu, S., McVeigh, J. A., Becerra, R., Bucks, R. S., Hunter, M., and Naragon-Gainey, K. 2024. "Repetitive Negative Thinking and Emotion Regulation as Mediators of the Association between Activity-Related Behaviours and Depression." *Journal of Affective Disorders Reports* 16, 100748. doi.org/10.1016/j.jadr.2024.100748.

Ludyga, S., Gerber, M., Pühse, U., Looser, V. N., and Kamijo, K. 2020. "Systematic Review and Meta-Analysis Investigating Moderators of Long-Term Effects of Exercise on Cognition in Healthy Individuals." *Nature Human Behaviour* 4 (6): 603–612. doi.org/10.1038/s41562-020-0851-8.

Mansueto, G., Marino, C., Palmieri, S., Offredi, A., Sarracino, D., Sassaroli, S., Ruggiero, G. M., Spada, M. M., and Caselli, G. 2022. "Difficulties in Emotion Regulation: The Role of Repetitive Negative Thinking and Metacognitive Beliefs." *Journal of Affective Disorders* 308, 473–483. doi.org/10.1016/j.jad.2022.04.086.

Mendes, C. G., Diniz, L. A., Marques Miranda, D. 2021. "Does Music Listening Affect Attention? A Literature Review." *Developmental Neuropsychology*. DOI: 10.1080/87565641.2021.1905816.

Mücke, M., Ludyga, S., Colledge, F., and Gerber, M. 2018. "Influence of Regular Physical Activity and Fitness on Stress Reactivity as Measured with the Trier Social Stress Test Protocol: A Systematic Review." *Sports Medicine* (Auckland, NZ) 48 (11): 2607–2622. doi.org/10.1007/s40279-018-0979-0.

Prakash, R. S. 2021. "Mindfulness Meditation: Impact on Attentional Control and Emotion Dysregulation." *Archives of Clinical Neuropsychology* 36 (7): 1283–1290.

Querstret, D., and Cropley, M. 2013. "Assessing Treatments Used to Reduce Rumination and/or Worry: A Systematic Review." *Clinical Psychology Review* 33 (8): 996–1009. doi.org/10.1016 /j.cpr.2013.08.004.

Severs, L. J., Vlemincx, E., and Ramirez, J. M. 2022. "The Psychophysiology of the Sigh: I: The Sigh from the Physiological Perspective." *Biological Psychology* 170: 108313.

Tseng, J., and Poppenk, J. 2020. "Brain Meta-State Transitions Demarcate Thoughts across Task Contexts Exposing the Mental Noise of Trait Neuroticism." *Nature Communications* 11 (1): 1–12. doi.org/10.1038/s41467-020-17255-9.

Vlemincx, E., Severs, L., and Ramirez, J. M. 2022. "The Psychophysiology of the Sigh: II: The Sigh from the Psychological Perspective." *Biological Psychology*, 108386.

Watkins, E. R. 2008. "Constructive and Unconstructive Repetitive Thought." *Psychological Bulletin* 134 (2): 163.

Watkins, E. R., and Roberts, H. 2020. "Reflecting on Rumination: Consequences, Causes, Mechanisms, and Treatment of Rumination." *Behaviour Research and Therapy* 127: 103573. doi.org/10.1016/j.brat.2020.103573.

Chapter Two

Bobba-Alves, N., Juster, R., and Picard, M. 2022. "The Energetic Cost of Allostasis and Allostatic Load." *Psychoneuroendocrinology* 146, 105951. doi.org/10.1016/j.psyneuen.2022.105951.

Curry, O. S., Rowland, L. A., Van Lissa, C. J., Zlotowitz, S., McAlaney, J., and Whitehouse, H. 2018. "Happy to Help? A Systematic Review and Meta-Analysis of the Effects of Performing Acts of Kindness on the Well-Being of the Actor." *Journal of Experimental Social Psychology* 76: 320–329. doi.org/10.1016/j.jesp.2018.02.014.

Fisher, K., Seidler, Z. E., King, K., Oliffe, J. L., and Rice, S. M. 2021. "Men's Anxiety: A Systematic Review." *Journal of Affective Disorders* 295: 688–702. doi.org/10.1016/j.jad.2021.08.136.

Gortner, E., Rude, S. S., and Pennebaker, J. W. 2006. "Benefits of Expressive Writing in Lowering Rumination and Depressive Symptoms." *Behavior Therapy* 37 (3): 292–303. doi.org/10.1016/j.beth.2006.01.004.

Grant, H. 2018. *Reinforcements: How to Get People to Help You.* Harvard Business Review Press.

Jamieson, J. P., Nock, M. K., and Mendes, W. B. 2012. "Mind over Matter: Reappraising Arousal Improves Cardiovascular and Cognitive Responses to Stress." *Journal of Experimental Psychology. General* 141 (3): 417. doi.org/10.1037/a0025719.

Lazar, L., and Eisenberger, N. I. 2022. "The Benefits of Giving: Effects of Prosocial Behavior on Recovery from Stress." *Psychophysiology* 59 (2): e13954. doi.org/10.1111/psyp.13954.

Lopes, S., Lima, M., and Silva, K. 2020. "Nature Can Get It out of Your Mind: The Rumination Reducing Effects of Contact with Nature and the Mediating Role of Awe and Mood." *Journal of Environmental Psychology* 71, article 101489. doi.org/10.1016/j.jenvp.2020.101489.

Niles, A. N., Haltom, K. E., Mulvenna, C. M., Lieberman, M. D., Stanton, A. L. 2014. "Randomized Controlled Trial of Expressive Writing for Psychological and Physical Health: The Moderating Role of Emotional Expressivity." *Anxiety Stress Coping* 27 (1): 1–17. DOI: 10.1080/10615806.2013.802308. Erratum in: *Anxiety Stress Coping* 27 (1): I.

Oveis, C., Gu, Y., Ocampo, J. M., Hangen, E. J., and Jamieson, J. P. 2020. "Emotion Regulation Contagion: Stress Reappraisal Promotes Challenge Responses in Teammates." *Journal of Experimental Psychology: General* 149 (11): 2187–2205. doi.org/10.1037/xge0000757.

Ozbay, F., Johnson, D. C., Dimoulas, E., Charney, D., and Southwick, S. 2007. "Social Support and Resilience to Stress: From Neurobiology to Clinical Practice." *Psychiatry* (Edgmont) 4 (5): 35–40. ncbi.nlm.nih.gov/pmc/articles/PMC2921311.

Pennebaker, J. W., and Chung, C. K. 2011. "Expressive Writing: Connections to Physical and Mental Health." In H. S. Friedman (ed.), *The Oxford Handbook of Health Psychology*. Oxford University Press (pp. 417–437).

Raposa, E. B., Laws, H. B., and Ansell, E. B. 2016. "Prosocial Behavior Mitigates the Negative Effects of Stress in Everyday Life." *Clinical Psychological Science* 4 (4): 691–698. doi.org/10.1177/2167702 615611073.

Reid, C., Rieves, E., and Carlson, K. 2022. "Perceptions of Green Space Usage, Abundance, and Quality of Green Space Were Associated with Better Mental Health during the Covid-19 Pandemic among Residents of Denver." *PLOS ONE* 17. doi.org/10.1371/journal.pone.0263779.

Riepenhausen, A., Wackerhagen, C., Reppmann, Z. C., Deter, C., Kalisch, R., Veer, I. M., and Walter, H. 2022. "Positive Cognitive Reappraisal in Stress Resilience, Mental Health, and Well-Being: A Comprehensive Systematic Review." *Emotion Review*. doi.org/10.1177/17540739221114642.

Sih, G., and Tang, K. 2013. "On–Off Switching of Theta–Delta Brain Waves Related to Falling Asleep and Awakening." *Theoretical and Applied Fracture Mechanics* 63–64: 1–17. doi.org/10.1016 /j.tafmec.2013.03.001.

Ullrich, P. M., and Lutgendorf, S. K. 2002. "Journaling about Stressful Events: Effects of Cognitive Processing and Emotional Expression." *Annals of Behavioral Medicine* 24 (3): 244–250. doi.org/10.1207/S15324796ABM2403_10.

Wapner, J. 2021. "Vision and Breathing May Be the Secrets to Surviving 2020." *Scientific American*. scientificamerican.com /article/vision-and-breathing-may-be-the-secrets-to -surviving-2020.

Zhao, X., and Epley, N. 2022. "Surprisingly Happy to Have Helped: Underestimating Prosociality Creates a Misplaced Barrier to Asking for Help." *Psychological Science*. doi.org/10.1177 /09567976221097615.

Chapter Three

Brailovskaia, J., Stirnberg, J., Rozgonjuk, D., Margraf, J., and Elhai, J. D. 2021. "From Low Sense of Control to Problematic Smartphone Use Severity during Covid-19 Outbreak: The Mediating Role of Fear of Missing Out and the Moderating Role of Repetitive Negative Thinking." *PLOS ONE* 16 (12): e0261023. doi.org/10.1371/journal.pone.0261023.

Carney, C. E., and Waters, W. F. 2006. "Effects of a Structured Problem-Solving Procedure on Pre-Sleep Cognitive Arousal in College Students with Insomnia." *Behavioral Sleep Medicine* 4 (1): 13–28. doi.org/10.1207/s15402010bsm0401_2.

Chaput, J. P., Dutil, C., Featherstone, R., Ross, R., Giangregorio, L., Saunders, T. J., Janssen, I., Poitras, V. J., Kho, M. E., Ross-White, A., Zankar, S., and Carrier, J. 2020. "Sleep Timing, Sleep Consistency, and Health in Adults: A Systematic Review." *Applied Physiology, Nutrition, and Metabolism = Physiologie appliquee, nutrition et metabolisme* 45 (10 [Suppl. 2]): S232–S247. doi.org/10.1139/apnm-2020-0032.

Cox, R. C., Cole, D. A., Kramer, E. L., and Olatunji, B. O. 2018. "Prospective Associations between Sleep Disturbance and Repetitive Negative Thinking: The Mediating Roles of Focusing and Shifting Attentional Control." *Behavior Therapy* 49 (1): 21–31. doi.org/10.1016/j.beth.2017.08.007.

Harris, R. 2008. *The Happiness Trap: How to Stop Struggling and Start Living*. Trumpeter Books.

Edinger, J. D., and Carney, C. E. 2014. *Overcoming Insomnia*. Oxford University Press.

Epton, T., Currie, S., and Armitage, C. J. 2017. "Unique Effects of Setting Goals on Behavior Change: Systematic Review and Meta-Analysis." *Journal of Consulting and Clinical Psychology* 85 (12): 1182–1198. doi.org/10.1037/ccp0000260.

Festinger, L. 1957. *A Theory of Cognitive Dissonance*. Stanford University Press.

Fogg, B. J. April 2009. "A Behavior Model for Persuasive Design." In *Proceedings of the 4th International Conference on Persuasive Technology* (pp. 1–7).

Harkin, B., Webb, T. L., Chang, B. P., Prestwich, A., Conner, M., Kellar, I., Benn, Y., and Sheeran, P. 2016. "Does Monitoring Goal Progress Promote Goal Attainment? A Meta-Analysis of the Experimental Evidence." *Psychological Bulletin* 142 (2): 198–229. doi.org/10.1037/bul0000025.

Jansson-Fröjmark, M., Lind, M., and Sunnhed, R. 2012. "Don't Worry, Be Constructive: A Randomized Controlled Feasibility Study Comparing Behaviour Therapy Singly and Combined with Constructive Worry for Insomnia." *British Journal of Clinical Psychology* 51 (2): 142–157. doi.org/10.1111/j.2044-8260 .2011.02018.x.

Kemp, J. 2021. *The ACT Workbook for Perfectionism: Build Your Best (Imperfect) Life Using Powerful Acceptance and Commitment Therapy and Self-Compassion Skills*. New Harbinger Publications.

Leroy, S. 2009. "Why Is It So Hard to Do My Work? The Challenge of Attention Residue When Switching between Work Tasks." *Organizational Behavior and Human Decision Processes* 109 (2): 168–181. doi.org/10.1016/j.obhdp.2009.04.002.

Rampton, J. 2019. "Time Blocking Tips Top Experts and Scientists Use to Increase Productivity." eliteescrowcoaching.com /wp-content/uploads/2019/05/May-2019-Article-of-the -Month-Time-Blocking-Tips-Top-Experts-and-Scientists-Use -to-Increase-Productivity.pdf.

Scullin, M. K., Krueger, M. L., Ballard, H. K., Pruett, N., and Bliwise, D. L. 2018. "The Effects of Bedtime Writing on Difficulty Falling Asleep: A Polysomnographic Study Comparing To-Do Lists and Completed Activity Lists." *Journal of Experimental Psychology. General* 147 (1): 139–146. doi.org/10.1037/xge0000374.

Takano, K., Sakamoto, S., and Tanno, Y. 2014. "Repetitive Thought Impairs Sleep Quality: An Experience Sampling Study." *Behavior Therapy* 45 (1): 67–82. doi.org/10.1016/j.beth.2013.09.004.

Walser, R. D., O'Connell, M., and Coulter, C. 2019. *The Heart of ACT: Developing a Flexible, Process-Based, and Client-Centered Practice Using Acceptance and Commitment Therapy.* Context Press.

Watkins, E. R., and Roberts, H. 2020. "Reflecting on Rumination: Consequences, Causes, Mechanisms, and Treatment of Rumination." *Behaviour Research and Therapy* 127: 103573. doi.org/10.1016/j.brat.2020.103573.

Wilson, K. G., and Murrell, A. R. 2004. "Values Work in Acceptance and Commitment Therapy: Setting a Course for Behavioral Treatment." In S. C. Hayes, V. M. Follette, and M. M. Linehan (eds.), *Mindfulness and Acceptance: Expanding the Cognitive Behavioral Tradition.* Guilford Press (pp. 120–151).

Wilson, K. G., Sandoz, E. K., Kitchens, J., and Roberts, M. 2010. "The Valued Living Questionnaire: Defining and Measuring Valued Action within a Behavioral Framework." *The Psychological Record* 60 (2): 249–272. doi.org/10.1007/BF03395706.

Zagaria, A., Ottaviani, C., Lombardo, C., and Ballesio, A. 2022.
"Perseverative Cognition as a Mediator between Perceived Stress
and Sleep Disturbance: A Structural Equation Modeling Meta-
Analysis (Meta-SEM)." *Annals of Behavioral Medicine: A
Publication of the Society of Behavioral Medicine*. doi.org/10.1093
/abm/kaac064.

Chapter Four

Bai, Y., Maruskin, L. A., Chen, S., Gordon, A. M., Stellar, J. E.,
McNeil, G. D., Peng, K., and Keltner, D. 2017. "Awe, the
Diminished Self, and Collective Engagement: Universals and
Cultural Variations in the Small Self." *Journal of Personality
and Social Psychology* 113 (2): 185–209. doi.org/10.1037
/pspa0000087.

Benkley, D., Willroth, E. C., Ayduk, O., John, O. P., and Mauss, I. B.
2023. "Short-Term Implications of Long-Term Thinking:
Temporal Distancing and Emotional Responses to Daily
Stressors." *Emotion* 23 (2): 595–599. doi.org/10.1037
/emo0001140.

Bruehlman-Senecal, E., and Ayduk, O. 2015. "This Too Shall Pass:
Temporal Distance and the Regulation of Emotional Distress."
Journal of Personality and Social Psychology 108 (2): 356–375.
doi.org/10.1037/a0038324.

Bruehlman-Senecal, E., Ayduk, Ö., and John, O. P. 2016. "Taking the
Long View: Implications of Individual Differences in Temporal
Distancing for Affect, Stress Reactivity, and Well-Being." *Journal
of Personality and Social Psychology* 111 (4): 610–635.
doi.org/10.1037/pspp0000103.

Brysbaert, M., Stevens, M., Mandera, P., and Keuleers, E. 2016. "How
Many Words Do We Know? Practical Estimates of Vocabulary
Size Dependent on Word Definition, the Degree of Language
Input and the Participant's Age." *Frontiers in Psychology* 7:
190735. doi.org/10.3389/fpsyg.2016.01116.

Burns, D. D. 1980. *Feeling Good: The New Mood Therapy*. Morrow.

Griskevicius, V., Shiota, M. N., and Neufeld, S. L. 2010. "Influence of Different Positive Emotions on Persuasion Processing: A Functional Evolutionary Approach." *Emotion* (Washington, DC) 10 (2): 190–206. doi.org/10.1037/a0018421.

Grossmann, I., and Kross, E. 2014. "Exploring Solomon's Paradox: Self-Distancing Eliminates the Self-Other Asymmetry in Wise Reasoning about Close Relationships in Younger and Older Adults." *Psychological Science* 25 (8): 1571–1580. doi.org/10.1177/0956797614535400.

Guo, L. 2022. "Reflect on Emotional Events from an Observer's Perspective: A Meta-Analysis of Experimental Studies." *Cognition & Emotion* 36 (8): 1531–1554. doi.org/10.1080/02699931.2022.2134094.

Hayes, S. C. 2005. *Get Out of Your Mind and Into Your Life: The New Acceptance and Commitment Therapy*. New Harbinger Publications (p. 80).

Huynh, A. C., Yang, J., and Grossmann, I. 2016. "The Value of Prospective Reasoning for Close Relationships." *Social Psychological and Personality Science*. doi.org/10.1177/1948550616660591.

Keltner, D. 2023. *Awe*. National Geographic Books.

Kross, E., and Ayduk, O. 2008. "Facilitating Adaptive Emotional Analysis: Distinguishing Distanced-Analysis of Depressive Experiences from Immersed-Analysis and Distraction." *Personality & Social Psychology Bulletin* 34 (7): 924–938. doi.org/10.1177/0146167208315938.

Kross, E., and Ayduk, O. 2017. "Self-Distancing: Theory, Research, and Current Directions." In Olson J., Zanna M. P. (eds), *Advances in Experimental Social Psychology* (vol. 55, pp. 81–136). Academic Press.

Larsson, A., Hooper, N., Osborne, L. A., Bennett, P., and McHugh, L. 2015. "Using Brief Cognitive Restructuring and Cognitive Defusion Techniques to Cope with Negative Thoughts." *Behavior Modification*. doi.org/10.1177/0145445515621488.

Masuda, A., Hayes, S. C., Sackett, C. F., and Twohig, M. P. 2004. "Cognitive Defusion and Self-Relevant Negative Thoughts: Examining the Impact of a Ninety-Year-Old Technique." *Behaviour Research and Therapy* 42 (4): 477–485. doi.org/10.1016/j.brat.2003.10.008.

Monroy, M., and Keltner, D. 2023. "Awe as a Pathway to Mental and Physical Health." *Perspectives on Psychological Science* 18 (2): 309–320. doi.org/10.1177/17456916221094856.

Orvell, A., Bruehlman-Senecal, E., Vickers, B., Kross, E., and Ayduk, Ö. 2023. "From the Laboratory to Daily Life: Preliminary Evidence That Self-Distancing Training Buffers Vulnerable Individuals against Daily Rumination and Depression over Time." *Psychology of Consciousness: Theory, Research, and Practice* 10 (2): 164–180. doi.org/10.1037/cns0000323.

Paquette, J. 2020. *Awestruck*. Shambhala Publications.

Powers, J. P., and LaBar, K. S. 2019. "Regulating Emotion through Distancing: A Taxonomy, Neurocognitive Model, and Supporting Meta-Analysis." *Neuroscience and Biobehavioral Reviews* 96: 155–173. doi.org/10.1016/j.neubiorev.2018.04.023.

Titchener, E. B. 1916. "Pickle, Pickle, Pickle." Adapted from Titchener, E. B. (1916). *A Beginner's Guide to Psychology*. Macmillan.

Van der Weel, F. R., and Van der Meer, A.L.H. 2024. "Handwriting but Not Typewriting Leads to Widespread Brain Connectivity: A High-Density EEG Study with Implications for the Classroom." *Frontiers in Psychology*. 14: 1219945. DOI: 10.3389/fpsyg.2023.1219945.

Wang, Y., Vantieghem, I., Dong, D., Nemegeer, J., Mey, J. D., Schuerbeek, P. V., Marinazzo, D., and Vandekerckhove, M. 2022. "Approaching or Decentering? Differential Neural Networks Underlying Experiential Emotion Regulation and Cognitive Defusion." *Brain Sciences* 12 (9) doi.org/10.3390/brainsci 12091215.

White, R. E., Kuehn, M. M., Duckworth, A. L., Kross, E., and Ayduk, Ö. 2019. "Focusing on the Future from Afar: Self-Distancing from Future Stressors Facilitates Adaptive Coping." *Emotion* 19 (5): 903–916. doi.org/10.1037/emo0000491.

Chapter Five

Balban, M. Y., Neri, E., Kogon, M. M., Weed, L., Nouriani, B., Jo, B., Holl, G., Zeitzer, J. M., Spiegel, D., and Huberman, A. D. 2023. "Brief Structured Respiration Practices Enhance Mood and Reduce Physiological Arousal." *Cell Reports Medicine* 4 (1): 100895. doi.org/10.1016/j.xcrm.2022.100895.

Bentley, T. G., Rakic, M., Arce, N., LaFaille, M., Berman, R., Cooley, K., and Sprimont, P. 2023. "Breathing Practices for Stress and Anxiety Reduction: Conceptual Framework of Implementation Guidelines Based on a Systematic Review of the Published Literature." *Brain Sciences* 13 (12): 1612. doi.org/10.3390/brainsci13121612.

Bringman, H., Giesecke, K., Thörne, A., and Bringman, S. 2009. "Relaxing Music as Pre-Medication before Surgery: A Randomised Controlled Trial." *Acta Anaesthesiologica Scandinavica* 53 (6): 759–764. doi.org/10.1111/j.1399-6576.2009.01969.x.

Curran, T., and Hill, A. P. 2019. "Perfectionism Is Increasing over Time: A Meta-Analysis of Birth Cohort Differences from 1989 to 2016." *Psychological Bulletin* 145 (4): 410–429. doi.org/10.1037/bul0000138.

Killingsworth, M. A., and Gilbert, D. T. 2010. "A Wandering Mind Is an Unhappy Mind." *Science*. doi.org/1192439.

Lazar, L., and Eisenberger, N. I. 2022. "The Benefits of Giving: Effects of Prosocial Behavior on Recovery from Stress." *Psychophysiology* 59 (2): e13954. doi.org/10.1111/psyp.13954.

Linehan, M. M. 2014. *DBT Training Manual*. The Guilford Press.

Pew Research Center. "Key Findings about Online Dating in the US." February 2, 2023. pewresearch.org/short-reads/2023/02/02/key-findings-about-online-dating-in-the-u-s.

Price, M. M., Zanesco, A. P., Denkova, E., Barry, J., Rogers, S. L., and Jha, A. P. 2023. "Investigating the Protective Effects of Mindfulness-Based Attention Training on Mind Wandering in Applied Settings." *Frontiers in Psychology* 14: 1232598. doi.org/10.3389/fpsyg.2023.1232598.

Price, V. H. 1999. "Treatment of Hair loss." *The New England Journal of Medicine* 341 (13): 964–973. doi.org/10.1056/NEJM199909233411307.

Steel, P. 2007. "The Nature of Procrastination: A Meta-Analytic and Theoretical Review of Quintessential Self-Regulatory Failure." *Psychological Bulletin* 133 (1): 65–94. doi.org/10.1037/0033-2909.133.1.65.

Thompson, D. February 14, 2024. "Why Americans Suddenly Stopped Hanging Out." *The Atlantic*. theatlantic.com/ideas/archive/2024/02/america-decline-hanging-out/677451.

Treynor, W., Gonzalez, R., and Nolen-Hoeksema, S. 2003. "Rumination Reconsidered: A Psychometric Analysis." *Cognitive Therapy and Research* 27 (3): 247–259.

Zinsser, N. 2022. *The Confident Mind: A Battle-Tested Guide to Unshakable Performance*. Portfolio.

Index

Acknowledgments

Thank you to my editor at Penguin Random House, Sarah Curley, for approaching me with this opportunity and expert guidance. Thank you to Bethany Reis, John Calmeyer, and Katy Brown for your production and design, which brought this book to life.

Thank you to my colleagues, who have put wind in my sails to write this book; the heart you put into your work is inspiring. Also, thank you to Vadim Albinsky, Peter Brown, and other friends who took the time to offer constructive feedback.

To my wife: you're an unsung hero. Your sacrifices amid the impossible balancing act of your career and parenting made this book a reality. And to my spirited daughters: thank you for grounding me. I'm awestruck by your imagination and silliness.

Mom: words can't capture your influence and love. I'd never be here had you not set me straight and believed in me each step of the way. To my big sister, you brilliantly lead the way and have modeled how to meet challenges.

Finally, to the men I've worked with in clinical settings each day, especially those who didn't inherit healthy versions of masculinity, it's an immense honor to witness you flip the script and soar.

About the Author

Dr. Jett Stone is a clinical psychologist, writer, and organizational consultant on a mission to improve men's mental well-being and add multidimensionality to their inner lives. Stone is also a Men's League hockey player past his prime and a dad to daughters, and he plays multiple instruments. Stone went to undergrad at the University of Michigan and earned two master's degrees in journalism and psychology from Columbia University. He completed his PhD in clinical psychology at Adelphi University and continued training at the Manhattan Veterans Affairs Hospital.

Stone eventually founded a clinical practice in Connecticut, focusing on individual and couples psychotherapy, and supervises doctoral students. As a consultant for Work Haven, Stone helps leaders thrive in their high-stress careers. He also writes for *Psychology Today*, where his articles focus on the male mind. His writings and contributions have appeared in academic journals, the *New York Times*, the *Guardian*, and *Fortune*.

Hi there,

We hope *Quiet Your Mind: A Men's Guide* helped you. If you have any questions or concerns about your book, or have received a damaged copy, please contact customerservice@penguinrandomhouse.com. We're here and happy to help.

Also, please consider writing a review on your favorite retailer's website to let others know what you thought of the book.

Sincerely,
The Zeitgeist Team